MAKING A DIFFERENCE
A STUDY OF THE EARLY CHRISTIANS IN THE BOOK OF ACTS

TIM CHRISTOSON

Copyright © 2009 by Striving Together Publications. All Scripture quotations are taken from the King James Version.

First published in 2009 by Striving Together Publications, a ministry of Lancaster Baptist Church, Lancaster, CA 93535. Striving Together Publications is committed to providing tried, trusted, and proven books that will further equip local churches to carry out the Great Commission. Your comments and suggestions are valued.

All rights reserved. No part of this book may be reproduced, stored in a retrieval system, or transmitted in any form or by any means—electronic, mechanical, photocopy, recording, or otherwise—without written permission of the publisher, except for brief quotations in printed reviews.

Striving Together Publications
4020 E. Lancaster Blvd.
Lancaster, CA 93535
800.201.7748

Cover design by Andrew Jones
Layout by Craig Parker
Special thanks to our proofreaders.

ISBN 978-1-59894-085-5

Printed in the United States of America

Table of Contents

How to Use This Curriculum v

Introduction ix

Lesson One—Relationships Make a Difference 1

Lesson Two—Caring Makes a Difference. 17

Lesson Three—The Spirit-Filled Life Makes a Difference 31

Lesson Four—Generosity Makes a Difference 47

Lesson Five—Faithfulness Makes a Difference. 63

Lesson Six—Teamwork Makes a Difference 79

Lesson Seven—A Witness Makes a Difference. 97

Lesson Eight—Encouragement Makes a Difference. 117

Lesson Nine—Giving Makes a Difference 133

Lesson Ten—Prayer Makes a Difference 151

Lesson Eleven—Missions Makes a Difference 167

Lesson Twelve—Co-Laborers Make a Difference 185

Lesson Thirteen—Commitment Makes a Difference 203

How to Use This Curriculum

Take a moment to familiarize yourself with the features of this *Striving Together* Sunday school curriculum:

Schedule

The lessons contained in this curriculum are undated, allowing you to begin and end the teaching series at any time. There are thirteen lessons that traditionally may be taught weekly any time of the year.

Student Edition Books

Companion books are available through *Striving Together Publications*. These contain:

- The outlines with blanks that students may fill in during the lessons

- Various Scripture quotations used throughout each lesson
- Introductory lesson overviews
- Study questions for review throughout the week
- A suggested memory verse for each lesson

These books are excellent tools for class members. We suggest ordering enough books for each class member plus additional copies for new members who enroll during the teaching series. Giving class members a study book encourages them to be faithful to class, provides them with a devotional tool for use throughout the week, and allows them to review material learned previously.

Key Verses

The verses from which the lessons originated are included at the beginning of each lesson so that you may read them through several times in prayerful preparation for class. Many teachers choose to memorize their key verses. We suggest that you use your own Bible for Scripture reading during the class hour and encourage your class members to do so as well.

Lesson Theme

Each lesson includes a theme statement that provides a brief lesson objective.

Lesson Overview

The overview section introduces the larger concept of the week's lesson. It is provided to acquaint you with the specific emphasis of each lesson, especially as it relates to previous lessons in the curriculum.

HOW TO USE THIS CURRICULUM

Teaching Outline

The abbreviated outline enables you to view the entire lesson at a glance to see how the contents fit together. Teaching with an organized outline increases the students' abilities to understand and remember the lesson content.

Introduction

Our pastor wisely said, "We must be different in order to make a difference." Being different involves change—implementing new behaviors and setting aside sin and weights. So where do we begin? To whom do we look for help?

We can learn from a group of people about whom it was said, they "have turned the world upside down" (Acts 17:6). This group was the first-century church—common men and women who rallied around an uncommon cause and demonstrated uncommon characteristics to make an amazing difference.

Throughout these thirteen lessons, we will examine their lives and legacies. We will uncover one characteristic each week that enabled them to make this amazing difference. And we will seek to examine our own lives to determine how we might implement these very characteristics—so that we too will make a difference!

LESSON ONE

Relationships Make a Difference

Key Verses

Acts 2:42–47

Lesson Theme

To make a difference, we must work at building and maintaining healthy relationships within the body of Christ.

Lesson Overview

In the closing verses of Acts 2, we gain insight into the relationships of the early believers. We learn that building and maintaining healthy relationships in the body of Christ is one way we will make a difference.

The New Testament Epistles contain over thirty specific instructions concerning our relationships to "one another" (Romans 12:10; Galatians 5:13; Ephesians 4:32). Relationships in the body were a major priority in the first-century church, and they should continue to be so today.

Teaching Outline

I. Steadfastness in Character
   A. A commitment to God's Word
   B. A commitment to gathering together
   C. A commitment to godly conduct

II. Sensitivity to Others
   A. We are to be gracious toward others.
   B. We are to be generous toward others.

III. Singleness of Heart
   A. Unity requires constant effort.
   B. Unity results in an effective witness.

LESSON ONE

Relationships Make a Difference

1st Church
= Day of Pent.
3,000

Text

Mr. Robert

Acts 2:42–47

Introduction

Rev'l

Relationships are what life is all about! More important than the balance of our bank accounts is the value of our relationships. More important than the entries in our medical charts is the health of our relationships. No other factor in life will produce more stress, create greater fulfillment, lead to more heartache, or arouse more joy than what happens in our relationships. *Relations in the body.*

Consider the difference relationships make within the local assembly. Being a part of the local church…

- Allows for forming genuine friendships, building healthy relationships, and receiving voluntary

3

accountability (Romans 16:1–6; James 5:16; Proverbs 27:17).

- Enables us to bear one another's burdens (Galatians 6:1–5,10; Ecclesiastes 4:9–10; Acts 4:32–37).

- Builds a prayer network for mutual intercession (Acts 12:5–12; Romans 15:30; 1 Timothy 2:1, 5:5).

- Places us under the spiritual protection of godly leaders (Hebrews 13:17; Acts 20:28–29).

Relationships within the local church provide us with benefits found nowhere else in the world! But whether we allow those relationships to deteriorate or whether we build and strengthen them is up to us.

The early Christians learned quickly how to strengthen one another. They depended on one another, encouraged one another, and developed relationships that truly made a difference.

Let's learn from the first-century believers *three characteristics of healthy relationships.*

I.   Steadfastness in Character   How-A

ACTS 2:42

42 And they continued stedfastly in the apostles' doctrine and fellowship, and in breaking of bread, and in prayers.

Healthy relationships develop as we "continue steadfastly." You can't have a relationship with someone who doesn't stick around!

"Added unto them," the expression used in Acts 2:41 regarding the day of Pentecost, is an early reference to church membership. We must understand that, as members of His body, we are not only *connected* to one another in membership,

Lesson One—Relationships Make a Difference

but we are also *committed* to one another in relationships. To become a member is to join arms with others of like faith. Together we join God in His redemptive work in this world.

Are you steadfast in your commitment to life's relationships? Notice three ways this kind of commitment is demonstrated.

A. A commitment to God's Word

Verse 42 tells us that these believers *"continued stedfastly in the apostles' doctrine."* Our pastor has said, "Doctrine is the glue that holds the church together." For us to truly *"walk together"* (Amos 3:3), we must agree on what we believe about God, His Word, and His Son. We must not only believe the right doctrine, but we must also continue in that doctrine through consistent, personal time in God's Word.

Job expressed his commitment to God's Word in this way:

> Membership in the local assembly is a commitment to a body of *doctrine*, to a body of *people*, and to the body of Christ.

JOB 23:12

12 Neither have I gone back from the commandment of his lips; I have esteemed the words of his mouth more than my necessary food.

Notice what the Lord said to Joshua as he assumed leadership of the nation of Israel:

JOSHUA 1:8

8 This book of the law shall not depart out of thy mouth; but thou shalt meditate therein day and night, that thou mayest observe to do according to all that is written therein:

for then thou shalt make thy way prosperous, and then thou shalt have good success.

B. A commitment to gathering together

Verse 42 also speaks of fellowship. Togetherness has always been a characteristic of God's people. Even in the Old Testament it was important to God that His people gather together to hear His Word.

DEUTERONOMY 31:12

12 Gather the people together, men, and women, and children, and thy stranger that is within thy gates, that they may hear, and that they may learn, and fear the LORD your God, and observe to do all the words of this law:

In the New Testament, God continued to emphasize the importance of gathering together on a regular basis.

HEBREWS 10:25

25 Not forsaking the assembling of ourselves together, as the manner of some is; but exhorting one another: and so much the more, as ye see the day approaching.

Have you ever depended on someone who committed himself to a task, then neglected to complete it? I don't want people to wonder whether I'm going to be in my place, fulfilling my responsibility to the body. Solomon addressed the issue:

PROVERBS 25:19

19 Confidence in an unfaithful man in time of trouble is like a broken tooth, and a foot out of joint.

Determine to be faithful in church attendance!

LESSON ONE—RELATIONSHIPS MAKE A DIFFERENCE

C. A commitment to godly conduct

The nature of these relationships was one of sincere holiness. Verse 42 tells us they broke bread and prayed together. Even when sharing a meal, they found it natural to share in spiritual fellowship. Great friendships are those in which each friend strengthens the other in his spiritual walk—not just in prayer meetings, but in any setting.

PROVERBS 27:17

17 Iron sharpeneth iron; so a man sharpeneth the countenance of his friend.   Accountability

One sure way to diminish the quality of your relationships is to allow them to take on an unholy, worldly nature. Sometimes an immature Christian thinks that feeling relaxed enough to divulge gossip or engage in ungodly conversation with a friend is the sign of a deepening friendship. On the contrary, this type of communication is the first step toward a relationship's demise.

1 CORINTHIANS 15:33

33 Be not deceived: evil communications corrupt good manners.

A good friend is one who cares enough to confront, challenge, or correct you in humble sincerity when you need it.

PROVERBS 27:6

6 Faithful are the wounds of a friend; but the kisses of an enemy are deceitful.

II. Sensitivity to Others

ACTS 2:44–45

44 And all that believed were together, and had all things common;

45 And sold their possessions and goods, and parted them to all men, as every man had need.

Early Christians quickly found themselves in need. Some lost their livelihoods and the support of relatives when they chose to follow Christ. To whom could they turn but to their newfound family of believers? It's a good thing that these Christians were sensitive to one another's needs, or Christianity may never have made it to a second generation!

A. We are to be gracious toward others.

Thirty times in Paul's, Peter's, and John's letters, they used a form of the expression *grace to you* (Romans 1:7; 2 Thessalonians 1:2; Philemon 1:3; 1 Peter 1:2). Grace speaks of God's unmerited favor. These godly men desired God's very best for every person with whom they were connected. If they could be conduits to deliver that grace, they were glad to be used.

Paul challenged the Thessalonian believers to grow in their love toward one another.

1 THESSALONIANS 3:12

12 And the Lord make you to increase and abound in love one toward another, and toward all men, even as we do toward you:

Paul instructed the Galatians to bear one another's burdens and to look for opportunities to serve their fellow believers.

LESSON ONE—RELATIONSHIPS MAKE A DIFFERENCE

GALATIANS 6:2, 10

2 Bear ye one another's burdens, and so fulfil the law of Christ.

10 As we have therefore opportunity, let us do good unto all men, especially unto them who are of the household of faith.

This gracious behavior stands in contrast to our world where the tendency is to "look out for number one." Jesus illustrates this gracious behavior in the story of the Good Samaritan.

LUKE 10:33–34

33 But a certain Samaritan, as he journeyed, came where he was: and when he saw him, he had compassion on him,

34 And went to him, and bound up his wounds, pouring in oil and wine, and set him on his own beast, and brought him to an inn, and took care of him.

When you're gracious, you make a difference!

B. We are to be generous toward others.

The early Christians' generosity impelled them to sell their possessions and goods to meet one another's needs. We are not instructed in the New Testament to practice communal living, but we are to learn from and emulate the generous *spirit* of these Christians. We are unequivocally commanded to meet the needs of those around us when we are able to do so.

PROVERBS 3:27

27 Withhold not good from them to whom it is due, when it is in the power of thine hand to do it.

Those who have been blessed are cautioned to consider those around them. Since God is the originator

9

of my blessings, I must be careful not to misappropriate blessings He has sent my way—blessings that were specifically intended to help one of His children.

1 Timothy 6:17–18

17 Charge them that are rich in this world, that they be not highminded, nor trust in uncertain riches, but in the living God, who giveth us richly all things to enjoy;
18 That they do good, that they be rich in good works, ready to distribute, willing to communicate;

The Apostles John and James were clear about our responsibility to share with others.

1 John 3:17

17 But whoso hath this world's good, and seeth his brother have need, and shutteth up his bowels of compassion from him, how dwelleth the love of God in him?

James 2:15–16

15 If a brother or sister be naked, and destitute of daily food,
16 And one of you say unto them, Depart in peace, be ye warmed and filled; notwithstanding ye give them not those things which are needful to the body; what doth it profit?

When you are generous, you make a difference.

III.   Singleness of Heart

Acts 2:46–47

46 And they, continuing daily with one accord in the temple, and breaking bread from house to house, did eat their meat with gladness and singleness of heart,

LESSON ONE—RELATIONSHIPS MAKE A DIFFERENCE

47 Praising God, and having favour with all the people. And the Lord added to the church daily such as should be saved.

These verses paint a picture of a group of people who had sincere and unified hearts. These folks were not putting on a facade of politeness. They really cared for one another! They were thrilled not only about the cause that brought them together but also about the fellowship they shared.

A. Unity requires constant effort.

Unity does not happen accidentally! Maintaining unity requires great effort, humble hearts, thick skin, and a willingness to forgive. Abundant grace is required for God's people to go the distance with one another. This applies in family relationships, among friends, and in a church body.

Paul encouraged the Christians in Rome to work toward unity.

ROMANS 14:19

19 Let us therefore follow after the things which make for peace, and things wherewith one may edify another.

Our Lord knows that the daily grind of life takes its toll on relationships, and He gives clear instructions.

ROMANS 12:16–21

16 Be of the same mind one toward another. Mind not high things, but condescend to men of low estate. Be not wise in your own conceits.
17 Recompense to no man evil for evil. Provide things honest in the sight of all men.
18 If it be possible, as much as lieth in you, live peaceably with all men.

19 Dearly beloved, avenge not yourselves, but rather give place unto wrath: for it is written, Vengeance is mine; I will repay, saith the Lord.

20 Therefore if thine enemy hunger, feed him; if he thirst, give him drink: for in so doing thou shalt heap coals of fire on his head.

21 Be not overcome of evil, but overcome evil with good.

The key to unity is not finding perfect people. The only people we have to choose from are flawed! The key is working day in and day out at the relationships God has placed in our lives with imperfect people.

B. Unity results in an effective witness.

It is no coincidence that these gracious, generous, unified Christians had favor with onlookers. People who needed God took note of the grace-filled relationships that existed among the followers of Christ.

Before some were willing to accept the Christians' message, they needed to see that the Christians were real—that, though they also had difficulties and failures, they didn't hold grudges or keep score. And when onlookers saw their love and unity, they concluded, "That's what I'm looking for!"

> *"To dwell above with saints we love; won't that be glory! But to dwell below with saints we know; well, that's another story!"*
> —Warren Wiersbe

Jesus said that our love for one another would confirm to this world that we are His followers.

JOHN 13:35

35 By this shall all men know that ye are my disciples, if ye have love one to another.

LESSON ONE—RELATIONSHIPS MAKE A DIFFERENCE

In the face of widespread opposition and skepticism, Peter encouraged the early Christians to cultivate a godly testimony.

1 PETER 2:11–12

11   *Dearly beloved, I beseech you as strangers and pilgrims, abstain from fleshly lusts, which war against the soul;*

12   *Having your conversation honest among the Gentiles: that, whereas they speak against you as evildoers, they may by your good works, which they shall behold, glorify God in the day of visitation.*

D. Bonhoffer - Thankful, for our relationships, dont take them for granted

Conclusion

We need one another! The Christian life cannot be lived in isolation. God created us to relate to one another and to function interdependently.

Mr. Roberts ⇒ real church fellowship
Knox - open door policy

ECCLESIASTES 4:9–10

9   *Two are better than one; because they have a good reward for their labour.*

10   *For if they fall, the one will lift up his fellow: but woe to him that is alone when he falleth; for he hath not another to help him up.*

Without healthy relationships, we have no ministry—inside or outside the church. We must value our relationships. We must be steadfast in our commitment to Christ and one another. We must be sensitive to the lives and needs of those around us. And we must cultivate and protect a singleness of heart. In so doing, the world around us will see and know that our message of *another* relationship—a relationship with Christ—is real. Then, we'll truly make a difference.

Hopefully this helps us see areas to work on, get back to your good works.

Study Questions

1. What is more important than wealth or health?
   Relationships

2. Name a few benefits of being part of a local church.
   Forming genuine friendships, building healthy relationships, and receiving voluntary accountability

   Burdens are shared and loads are lightened

   Prayer network, for mutual intercession

   Places us under the spiritual protection of godly leaders

3. What are three characteristics of a healthy relationship?
   Steadfastness in character

   Sensitivity to others

   Singleness of heart

4. In Job 23:12, how necessary did Job say his commitment to God's Word was?
   More than my necessary food

5. What does Proverbs 25:19 say about having confidence in an unfaithful man?
   Like a broken tooth and a foot out of joint

6. First Corinthians 15:33 says that it is possible for good manners to be corrupted by evil communications. What are some things that would bring about corruption in a relationship?
   Answers will vary. Gossip, criticizing others, cursing, engaging in ungodly conversation

LESSON ONE—RELATIONSHIPS MAKE A DIFFERENCE

7. What is grace?
    God's unmerited favor

8. The story in Luke 10:33–34 portrays the gracious behavior of the Good Samaritan, illustrating what the Lord expects from His followers. What would you do in that situation? Name three ways you can be gracious toward someone this week.
    Answers will vary.

9. According to 1 John 3:17, what kind of conduct exposes a heart destitute of God's love?
    Not showing compassion

10. What does unity require?
    Constant effort

11. What characteristic evidences to others that we are Christ's followers?
    Our love for one another

Memory Verse

ROMANS 14:19
19 Let us therefore follow after the things which make for peace, and things wherewith one may edify another.

LESSON TWO

Caring Makes a Difference

Key Verses

Acts 3:1–10

Lesson Theme

To make a difference, we must demonstrate the care and concern of Jesus Christ to those in need.

Lesson Overview

Although caring for others does not come naturally, Spirit-filled believers of the first century cared not only for each other but also for those outside the walls of the church.

Peter and John serve as examples of compassionate Christians. They represented their Saviour well as they reached out in love and care to one who could offer them nothing in return. God was glorified by their demonstration of care, as He is glorified today when we look beyond our own needs to the needs of others.

Teaching Outline

I. The Plight of the Needy Man
    A. He needed strength to walk.
    B. He needed substance for living.
    C. He needed someone to care.

II. The Pity of the Caring Men
    A. Caring eyes to look at the man
    B. Caring hands to lift the man

III. The Praise of the Healed Man
    A. His praise was a witness of God's power.
    B. His praise was watched by the people.

LESSON TWO

Caring Makes a Difference

Text

Acts 3:1–10

Introduction

We have learned from the first generation Christians that healthy relationships make a difference. In this lesson we will learn from the example of early church leaders that caring makes a difference.

When Paul wrote the believers in Philippi, he spoke highly of two caring men, Timothy and Epaphroditus. They were among his small group of loyal helpers. Paul lamented the lack of similar men who would *"naturally care for"* the well-being of those in Philippi (Philippians 2:20).

We need to exercise care for others. From this scene in the lives of two early church members, we see *three components of genuine care.*

I.   The Plight of the Needy Man
ACTS 3:2

2   And a certain man lame from his mother's womb was carried, whom they laid daily at the gate of the temple which is called Beautiful, to ask alms of them that entered into the temple;

The inconvenient reality is that the opportunity to care always begins with a need. We tend to avoid needs because, after all, we have needs of our own. Our actions seem to say, "Don't bother me with needy people, because I am one!"

But if we strive to make a difference, we will express care for others. This man had at least three dire needs:

A.   He needed strength to walk.

He was simply lying there, helplessly sick—much like the people around us who are diseased with sin and morally crippled. Increasingly, we find ourselves repulsed by the depravity of this world.

The prophet Isaiah graphically portrayed mankind's sinful condition using the imagery of physical disease and decay.

ISAIAH 1:4–6

4   Ah sinful nation, a people laden with iniquity, a seed of evildoers, children that are corrupters: they have forsaken the LORD, they have provoked the Holy One of Israel unto anger, they are gone away backward.

LESSON TWO—CARING MAKES A DIFFERENCE

5   Why should ye be stricken any more? ye will revolt more and more: the whole head is sick, and the whole heart faint.
6   From the sole of the foot even unto the head there is no soundness in it; but wounds, and bruises, and putrifying sores: they have not been closed, neither bound up, neither mollified with ointment.

This is not a new scenario. Since Adam men have been *"dead in trespasses and sins"* (Ephesians 2:1). How can we expect men who do not know God to have moral health or strength? The fact that people are without strength is precisely why Jesus came!

ROMANS 5:6
6   For when we were yet without strength, in due time Christ died for the ungodly.

B. He needed substance for living.

This crippled man was asking for alms. He needed financial assistance to meet the needs in his life since he was physically unable to earn an income.

We also will meet people who have physical needs. Though we cannot meet every need, God may lead us to meet specific needs. Jesus spoke of the importance of a caring spirit.

MATTHEW 25:37–40
37   Then shall the righteous answer him, saying, Lord, when saw we thee an hungred, and fed thee? or thirsty, and gave thee drink?
38   When saw we thee a stranger, and took thee in? or naked, and clothed thee?
39   Or when saw we thee sick, or in prison, and came unto thee?

40 And the King shall answer and say unto them, Verily I say unto you, Inasmuch as ye have done it unto one of the least of these my brethren, ye have done it unto me.

The local church meets needs like this—often behind the scenes—on a daily basis. It is common for a deacon, teacher, or other leader to visit a widow, a poverty-stricken soul, or another person in need and to provide some basic need of life—a bag of groceries, a heating bill, or even some clothing or shoes. By giving tithes and offerings through your local church, you help meet benevolent needs. Meeting physical needs is just one facet of the caring work of the local church. We should be thankful to be part of a local church that is carrying out this biblical imperative of caring.

PROVERBS 19:17
17 He that hath pity upon the poor lendeth unto the LORD; and that which he hath given will he pay him again.

C. He needed someone to care.

Among all those entering the temple that day, this man noticed Peter and John specifically. He no doubt caught the eyes of many temple-goers and encountered a variety of responses, but when he locked eyes with these two men, an expectant hope sprang up within him. Somehow he knew—at least he hoped—they would help.

More people than we realize are looking for a person to help—a person to care. God may desire to use you as just that person in someone's life this week. David described the feeling of hopelessness:

LESSON TWO—CARING MAKES A DIFFERENCE

PSALM 142:4

4 I looked on my right hand, and beheld, but there was no man that would know me: refuge failed me; no man cared for my soul.

Often, what folks think they need is far short of what God really knows they need. This man was hoping to receive some coins, but he was completely healed of his lifelong debilitation! People around us may think they need a new friend, a new mortgage, a new career, or a new church, but God knows their need is Him. And He may choose you as His messenger of care. Will you be that someone?

II. The Pity of the Caring Men

ACTS 3:6–7

6 Then Peter said, Silver and gold have I none; but such as I have give I thee: In the name of Jesus Christ of Nazareth rise up and walk.

7 And he took him by the right hand, and lifted him up: and immediately his feet and ankle bones received strength.

In Christ's parable on forgiveness, the master asked the unforgiving servant, "*Shouldest not thou also have had compassion on thy fellowservant, even as I had pity on thee?*" (Matthew 18:33). Jesus may ask us the same question: "I had pity on you. Shouldn't you have pity on others?"

Peter and John teach us what it takes to demonstrate this compassion.

A. Caring eyes to look at the man

Verse 4 describes Peter as "*fastening his eyes upon him.*"

23

MAKING A DIFFERENCE

> **DEFINITION**
>
> *The English word* pity *appears only once in the New Testament and comes from the Greek word* eleeo *(ἐλεέω pronounced el-eh-eh´-o). It is also translated* mercy *and* compassion. *In fact, it's the very same word used in Jude 22, "And of some have compassion, making a difference."*

Perhaps most of the folks to cross the lame man's path throughout the years did what came naturally—looked the other way. We too see a need such as this and naturally but tragically look the other way. We must retrain ourselves to truly see people for who they are.

When you look at people, what do you see? Some notice hairstyle, clothing, skin color, and (in some gang-related scenarios) the color of clothes. Still others immediately size up social or economic status.

But if we will make a difference, we must see people as Peter and John saw this man. We must see them as they truly are—men and women with eternal souls in need of a Saviour.

Jeremiah's caring eyes affected his heart, and because of this, we know him today as the weeping prophet.

LAMENTATIONS 3:51
51 Mine eye affecteth mine heart because of all the daughters of my city.

Similarly, when Jesus looked on the lost souls of men with caring eyes, He was moved with compassion.

MATTHEW 9:36
36 But when he saw the multitudes, he was moved with compassion on them, because they fainted, and were scattered abroad, as sheep having no shepherd.

Some of us are like the blind man before Jesus finished healing him, seeing men as less significant than they truly are. We need Christ's touch to enable us to see men "clearly."

MARK 8:24–25
24 And he looked up, and said, I see men as trees, walking.
25 After that he put his hands again upon his eyes, and made him look up: and he was restored, and saw every man clearly.

B. Caring hands to lift the man

Peter and John did more than experience emotion. They moved into action. They placed their hands on this man, gripped his feeble body, and helped him to his feet.

Think of this: God's power alone could certainly have enabled this man to stand to his feet without the assistance of Peter and John. But God helps those in need by using compassionate people who are willing to become personally involved.

This is the behavior of which Solomon spoke:

ECCLESIASTES 4:9–10
9 Two are better than one; because they have a good reward for their labour.
10 For if they fall, the one will lift up his fellow: but woe to him that is alone when he falleth; for he hath not another to help him up.

There are many things Jesus did that we cannot duplicate. We cannot raise the dead, walk on water, or cleanse lepers. We can, however, reach out our hands to lift up those in need. "He came and took her by the hand,

and lifted her up…" (Mark 1:31). *"Jesus took him by the hand, and lifted him up…"* (Mark 9:27).

When you lift someone up—when you care enough to get involved—you are, in that moment, like Jesus.

Whom have you lifted lately? A kind word can lift a person's spirit. A thoughtful act can lift a person's burden. Introducing a man to Jesus Christ can lift him right into an eternal relationship with God and a home in Heaven for eternity!

III. The Praise of the Healed Man

Acts 3:8

8 *And he leaping up stood, and walked, and entered with them into the temple, walking, and leaping, and praising God.*

He had never walked before, but now he could walk. He had never leapt before, but now he was leaping. He likely had never entered the temple before, but now he entered unassisted. And that's not all he was doing. He was also praising God!

A. His praise was a witness of God's power.

This man's first response to healing was to praise God. He wanted everyone to know that God had changed his life.

Ephesians 1:12

12 *That we should be to the praise of his glory, who first trusted in Christ.*

The testimony of a changed life is a wonderful tool. People can argue with our message. They can resist our reason. But they cannot deny the message of a transformed life.

LESSON TWO—CARING MAKES A DIFFERENCE

The skeptics find it hard to explain why someone doesn't talk the way he used to talk, go to the places he used to go, tell the jokes he used to tell, drink the substance he used to drink, or behave the way he used to behave. They can't argue with the fact that something (in reality, *Someone*) has changed his life from the inside out.

2 CORINTHIANS 5:17

17 Therefore if any man be in Christ, he is a new creature: old things are passed away; behold, all things are become new.

B. His praise was watched by the people.

ACTS 3:9–10

9 And all the people saw him walking and praising God: 10 And they knew that it was he which sat for alms at the Beautiful gate of the temple: and they were filled with wonder and amazement at that which had happened unto him.

Notice the words *all the people saw him*. This healed man didn't need to preach a sermon; he *was* the sermon! He just did what God had suddenly enabled him to do. Maybe you should do the same—be a sermon. Just do what God has enabled you to do. Show up to work on time, live with integrity, love your spouse, raise your children to be godly. Do the things that you couldn't do without Christ, and when people ask how you do them, say, "It's because of Him!"

Oh yes, and in case you're wondering, Peter did get around to preaching a sermon—in short order (see verses 12–26). But there wouldn't have been a crowd to preach to if the man hadn't leapt, walked, and praised

God. People were watching, and Peter was able to say
to them:

Acts 3:16
*16 And his name through faith in his name hath made
this man strong, whom ye see and know: yea, the faith
which is by him hath given him this perfect soundness in
the presence of you all.*

People who need God are watching how we handle
the ups and downs in the economy, how we deal with
bad news from the doctor, how we treat our family
members, and how we live day in and day out. Jesus said
that this "fish bowl" is a wonderful place to give glory to
our Father.

Matthew 5:16
*16 Let your light so shine before men, that they may
see your good works, and glorify your Father which is
in heaven.*

Conclusion

It's amazing what happens when people care. Because two
men slowed down and stopped for a lame man, because
they saw him—someone who didn't have anything to offer
them—and they cared: a man was healed, people heard the
Gospel message, and God received glory.

Will you care for the people whom God brings across
your path this week? Will you care enough to reach out to
them with God's love and to lift them toward the Saviour?

LESSON TWO—CARING MAKES A DIFFERENCE

Study Questions

1. Which two men in Philippians 2 did Paul commend for their compassion and care?
    Timothy and Epaphroditus

2. What were the three needs of the lame man in our lesson?
    Strength to walk

    Substance for living

    Someone to care

3. Are we, as Christians, commanded to meet only the spiritual needs of others? Please support your answer with a verse.
    As Christians, we are to meet not only the spiritual needs of others but the physical needs as well. Though we might not be able to meet every need, God may lead us to meet specific needs. Matthew 25:37–40 speaks of meeting legitimate, physical needs.

4. List some practical ways you could meet someone's physical need.
    Answers will vary.

5. What does the word *pity* mean?
    Mercy and compassion

6. In Matthew 9:36, what caused Jesus to be moved with compassion?
    The lost souls of men

7. In verse 7 of our text, Peter and John took the lame man by the hand and lifted him up. It would have done absolutely no good for them to just look at the man and feel bad. If we are going to make a difference, we must do more than see a need; we must be willing to do something about the need. Has the Lord put on your heart someone for whom you need to do more than feel sorry? If so, how should you respond?
Answers will vary.

8. What three things did the lame man do while entering the temple?
Walked, leaped, praised God

9. According to 2 Corinthians 5:17, what does a person become when he accepts Christ as his Saviour?
He is a new creature.

10. According to Matthew 5:16, how do we bring glory to God?
Answers will vary. We bring glory to God through our good works, including caring for others.

Memory Verse

MATTHEW 5:16
16 Let your light so shine before men, that they may see your good works, and glorify your Father which is in heaven.

LESSON THREE

The Spirit-Filled Life Makes a Difference

Key Verses

Acts 4:29–31

Lesson Theme

To make a difference, we must constantly seek to be filled with the Holy Spirit of God.

Lesson Overview

The book of Acts is often referred to as "The Acts of the Apostles." Someone once suggested that a more appropriate name would be "The Acts of the Holy Spirit" because every soul saved, every victory won, and every advancement made within the local church is accomplished only by the Holy Spirit's ministry.

In the closing verses of Acts 4, we observe in great detail the fullness of the Holy Spirit evidenced in believers' lives. May we follow their examples and expect God's Spirit to fill us, shape us, and use us today!

Teaching Outline

    I. The Priority of Being Filled with the Holy Spirit

        A. The Holy Spirit is our promise.

        B. The Holy Spirit is our power.

    II. The Pathway to Being Filled with the Holy Spirit

        A. Connect with God.

        B. Confess to God.

        C. Call on God.

        D. Continue with God.

    III. The Product of Being Filled with the Holy Spirit

        A. The Spirit produces a bold witness.

        B. The Spirit produces a steady walk.

        C. The Spirit produces a divine work.

LESSON THREE

The Spirit-Filled Life Makes a Difference

Text

Acts 4:29–31

Introduction

In our last lesson we learned from Peter and John's encounter with the lame man that caring makes a difference.

This lesson picks up where we left off. Oddly enough, the temple leaders weren't too happy that this man was now walking, leaping, and praising God. They were even less pleased with Peter's message to the crowd about the Lord Jesus Christ and His power to heal. (Some things don't change. Many people today don't mind religious talk, as long as it leaves Jesus out.)

How interesting that the preaching of the Gospel brings such a mixed response. As Acts 4 opens, we find Peter and John arrested by the temple leaders (vv. 1–3). At the same time, five thousand others embraced the message of salvation (v. 4)!

The day after their arrest, the high priest and his religious colleagues hauled Peter and John before the crowd and raised this question: *"By what power, or by what name, have ye done this?"*

The source of their power this day—and in the exciting days of ministry that lay ahead for these pioneering Christians—was the person of the Holy Spirit. And Peter wasn't the only one who was experiencing His fullness. Learn from Peter and the other faithful disciples *three perspectives on being filled with the Spirit.*

I. The Priority of Being Filled with the Holy Spirit

As the crowd gathered, Peter was given an opportunity to defend the faith of the Apostles. The single most important factor in this critical moment for the early church was not Peter's education, social connections, or financial resources. It was that Peter was filled with the Holy Spirit.

ACTS 4:8

8 *Then Peter, filled with the Holy Ghost, said unto them, Ye rulers of the people, and elders of Israel,*

The filling of the Holy Spirit is not needed just for preaching or for the work of the Apostles. His presence is necessary for every Christian, in all circumstances, each day.

For example, in Ephesians 5, the New Testament's classic chapter on the marriage relationship, the Apostle Paul begins his instructions to husbands and wives by commanding them to be filled with the Spirit.

Lesson Three—The Spirit-Filled Life

Ephesians 5:18

18 And be not drunk with wine, wherein is excess; but be filled with the Spirit;

A. The Holy Spirit is our promise.

In John 16, following the upper room supper, the Lord Jesus explained to His disciples that though He would be going away, He would send the Holy Spirit to teach, comfort, and guide them.

John 16:7

7 Nevertheless I tell you the truth; It is expedient for you that I go away: for if I go not away, the Comforter will not come unto you; but if I depart, I will send him unto you.

After His resurrection and before His ascension to Heaven, Jesus reminded them of this promise once again. In fact, Jesus explained that the Holy Spirit's ministry was so important they would need to wait in Jerusalem for His arrival.

"For the Christian, all ground is holy ground, and every bush is a burning bush."

—Vance Havner

Acts 1:4–5

4 And, being assembled together with them, commanded them that they should not depart from Jerusalem, but wait for the promise of the Father, which, saith he, ye have heard of me.

5 For John truly baptized with water; but ye shall be baptized with the Holy Ghost not many days hence.

MAKING A DIFFERENCE

B. The Holy Spirit is our power.

ACTS 1:8

8 *But ye shall receive power, after that the Holy Ghost is come upon you: and ye shall be witnesses unto me both in Jerusalem, and in all Judaea, and in Samaria, and unto the uttermost part of the earth.*

Through the ministry of the Holy Spirit, Jesus will share this divine power with His children, and they will be empowered for the express purpose of glorifying God.

DEFINITION

The word translated power *in Acts 1:8 is different from the word* power *used in other places, such as Matthew 28:18. The Greek word here is* dunamis *(δύναμις pronounced doo´-nam-is), from the word* dunamai *(δύναμαι prounounced doo´-nam-ahee). According to* Strong's, *dunamis means, "strength, miraculous power, abundant might, [attributed to a] worker of miracles [or to a] mighty (wonderful) work." It's the origin of our modern word* dynamite!

The Holy Spirit's power enables us to do what we cannot do in our own strength. His power enables us to be kind and sweet to our spouses though we've had a bad day. His power enables us to refuse sin though we're sorely tempted. His power enables us to forgive and restore though we've been wronged.

The only way we will ever accomplish anything of eternal significance or miraculous proportions is through the power of the Holy Spirit.

Experiencing His fullness is the highest and most urgent priority!

LESSON THREE—THE SPIRIT-FILLED LIFE

II. The Pathway to Being Filled with the Holy Spirit

Many other believers were filled with the Holy Spirit besides Peter. The fullness of the Spirit is not just for apostles, preachers, or missionaries. The Holy Spirit's filling was "standard operating procedure" for all first-century Christians.

ACTS 4:31

31 And when they had prayed, the place was shaken where they were assembled together; and they were all filled with the Holy Ghost, and they spake the word of God with boldness.

If you desire to be filled with the Holy Spirit, consider the following steps, which, if practiced daily, can enable you to experience the same power that those first-century Christians experienced.

A. Connect with God.

Give priority to spending time with God in prayer and Bible study. See what the observers noticed about Peter and John in this passage:

ACTS 4:13B

13B ...and they took knowledge of them, that they had been with Jesus.

The Holy Spirit's filling results from time spent with Jesus. If you haven't spent time with Him, you can't be filled by His Spirit.

JOHN 15:5

5 I am the vine, ye are the branches: He that abideth in me, and I in him, the same bringeth forth much fruit: for without me ye can do nothing.

37

Are you carving out time in your daily schedule to meet with God? Do you have an appointment with Him when you'll be alone and quiet—not rushed—in His presence, with an open Bible and a prayerful heart?

If you miss this time with Him, you will miss the fullness of the Holy Spirit. And if you miss the fullness of the Spirit, you will miss the major source of wisdom, power, comfort, and direction that God intended you to possess.

B. Confess to God.

Forsake the sin and weights that prevent the Spirit's fullness. To be filled with the Spirit, we must clear the way of obstacles and impediments which prevent the flow of His power and presence into our lives.

PSALM 66:18

18 If I regard iniquity in my heart, the Lord will not hear me:

ISAIAH 59:1–2

1 Behold, the LORD's hand is not shortened, that it cannot save; neither his ear heavy, that it cannot hear:
2 But your iniquities have separated between you and your God, and your sins have hid his face from you, that he will not hear.

You cannot be filled with God if you are already filled with self-will, stubborn sin, or a preoccupation with lesser things. We must empty ourselves of sin and come clean with God.

HEBREWS 12:1

1 Wherefore seeing we also are compassed about with so great a cloud of witnesses, let us lay aside every weight,

Lesson Three—The Spirit-Filled Life

and the sin which doth so easily beset us, and let us run with patience the race that is set before us,

Once you've established the connection with God and confessed, then…

C. Call on God.

If you want your Heavenly Father to bestow the Holy Spirit's presence and power in your life, ask!

Luke 11:13

13 If ye then, being evil, know how to give good gifts unto your children: how much more shall your heavenly Father give the Holy Spirit to them that ask him?

Take a moment each morning and ask God to empty you of self and fill you with His Spirit. Ask Him to replace your fleshly nature—pride, anger, fear, etc.—with His divine nature—humility, meekness, faith, etc. Ask Him to direct your words, actions, reactions, decisions, motives, and even your thoughts.

Die to self and give the Holy Spirit control.

Romans 6:6

6 Knowing this, that our old man is crucified with him, that the body of sin might be destroyed, that henceforth we should not serve sin.

Just as a flight suit or firefighter's gear is not controlled by itself but by the power of the body that fills it, our goal is not to be controlled by our bodies but by the Holy Spirit dwelling within us.

GALATIANS 2:20

20 I am crucified with Christ: nevertheless I live; yet not I, but Christ liveth in me: and the life which I now live in the flesh I live by the faith of the Son of God, who loved me, and gave himself for me.

This Spirit-controlled life is what the hymn writer, Frances Havergal, had in mind when she wrote the following hymn.

Hymn

Take My Life and Let it Be

Take my life and let it be
Consecrated Lord, to Thee;
Take my moments and my days—
Let them flow in ceaseless praise,
Let them flow in ceaseless praise.

Take my hands and let them move
At the impulse of Thy love;
Take my feet and let them be
Swift and beautiful for Thee,
Swift and beautiful for Thee.

Take my voice and let me sing
Always, only for my King;
Take my lips and let them be
Filled with messages from Thee,
Filled with messages from Thee.

Finally, when you rise up from your time of connecting, confessing, and calling on God to fill you, then you must...

LESSON THREE—THE SPIRIT-FILLED LIFE

D. Continue with God.

Walk through each day exercising sensitivity to God's leadership and following His direction. Unfortunately, a Spirit-filled life doesn't come automatically, even after spending time with God. Sometimes people who spend time with God in the morning are functioning in the flesh by afternoon.

We must walk in the Spirit, remaining sensitive to God's *"still small voice"* (1 Kings 19:12) within, and follow His leading throughout the day. You may have to pause a few hours into the day and whisper a prayer, asking for God's guidance, wisdom, and power. Walking in the Spirit might mean avoiding a tempting situation, refusing a sinful opportunity, or recalling a Scripture to help you make wise decisions.

GALATIANS 5:16

16 This I say then, Walk in the Spirit, and ye shall not fulfil the lust of the flesh.

PROVERBS 3:6

6 In all thy ways acknowledge him, and he shall direct thy paths.

III. The Product of Being Filled with the Holy Spirit

ACTS 4:29–30

29 And now, Lord, behold their threatenings: and grant unto thy servants, that with all boldness they may speak thy word,
30 By stretching forth thine hand to heal; and that signs and wonders may be done by the name of thy holy child Jesus.

41

A. The Spirit produces a bold witness.

ACTS 4:13

13 *Now when they saw the boldness of Peter and John, and perceived that they were unlearned and ignorant men, they marvelled; and they took knowledge of them, that they had been with Jesus.*

ACTS 4:31B

31B ...they were all filled with the Holy Ghost, and they spake the word of God with boldness.

The boldness that God wants us to exercise with His message does not come naturally. By nature we are not bold but hesitant to share the Gospel of Christ as we should. So we must receive the spiritual power and energy of the Holy Spirit to make us the bold witnesses Christ has called us to be.

> "Obey every impulse of the Holy Spirit."
>
> —Paul Chappell

Some attempt boldness in their own strength, but they mistake *brashness* with *boldness*.

The Holy Spirit gives boldness to witness when it's not convenient, to speak up when it's not easy, and to share our faith in the midst of opposition. We cannot win others to Christ and influence the lost without the Holy Spirit's boldness.

PROVERBS 28:1

1 *The wicked flee when no man pursueth: but the righteous are bold as a lion.*

B. The Spirit produces a steady walk.

ACTS 4:18–20

18 *And they called them, and commanded them not to speak at all nor teach in the name of Jesus.*

LESSON THREE—THE SPIRIT-FILLED LIFE

19 But Peter and John answered and said unto them, Whether it be right in the sight of God to hearken unto you more than unto God, judge ye.
20 For we cannot but speak the things which we have seen and heard.

In the face of threats, these men walked steadily. They weren't going to allow political, religious, or cultural pressure to cause them to cave.

How steady is your walk? Amid the shifting waves of philosophies and doctrines, may God enable His children to stand in contrast to these times and maintain a steady walk.

Can we remain steady? Yes, because the Holy Spirit, like an anchor, is keeping us where God would have us to be. Malachi 3:6 says it plainly: *"For I am the LORD, I change not...."* Hebrews 13:8 agrees: *"Jesus Christ the same yesterday, and to day, and for ever."*

C. The Spirit produces a divine work.

ACTS 4:30
30 By stretching forth thine hand to heal; and that signs and wonders may be done by the name of thy holy child Jesus.

These early Christians had just seen three thousand saved on Pentecost, followed by the healing of the lame man, then the salvation of five thousand more. But these early Christians were believing God for even greater miracles in the days ahead. How could they ask for such miraculous things? They understood that the Holy Spirit had come. And with the Holy Spirit's presence, anything is possible.

We should learn to trust God for more than we have ever trusted Him for and learn to ask for divine-caliber results. Why? The Holy Spirit is as able to work now as He was in the first century! If the results of our ministry can be explained by men's skills and abilities, we're landing far short of what God wants for us. We ought to learn to pray:

> Dear God, in my life (or in my ministry, family, career, or marriage) please accomplish so great a work that it is clear to all that You are at work here. May You so exceed my expectations, that the results are obviously a product of Your power, not mine.

This seems to be what Paul was driving at:

2 Corinthians 4:7
7   But we have this treasure in earthen vessels, that the excellency of the power may be of God, and not of us.

Conclusion

The Holy Spirit is Jesus Christ's promise to us. He is the source of our power. He came to live within you the moment you received God's gift of salvation. But on a daily basis you have the choice of whether or not you will do what is necessary to be filled and controlled by Him.

He can give you the power to witness, to overcome sin, and to make a difference in this world beyond your imagination. He can give you the power to love your spouse, raise your children, and impact the lives of others.

Will you connect with Him and then walk under His control each day?

LESSON THREE—THE SPIRIT-FILLED LIFE

Study Questions

1. Whom did Jesus tell His disciples He would send to comfort, teach, and guide them in His absence?
The Holy Spirit

2. In Ephesians 5:18, the Bible tells us not to be drunk with wine, but to be filled with the Spirit. Explain what this verse means.
The Holy Spirit is to completely control the Christian, just as alcohol controls a person.

3. In Acts 1:8, what is the Greek word for *power*, and what is its definition?
Dunamis *means strength, miraculous power, abundant might, [attributed to a] worker of miracles [or to a] mighty (wonderful) work.*

4. Is the fullness of the Spirit intended primarily for apostles, preachers, and missionaries?
No, for all who are saved

5. List the steps on the pathway to being filled with the Spirit.
Connect with God.

Confess to God.

Call on God.

Continue with God.

6. If you will be filled with the Spirit, what daily routine must be a major priority in your life?
Spending time with God in prayer and Bible study

MAKING A DIFFERENCE

7. According to Psalm 66:18, what prevents the Lord from hearing our prayers?
Sin in our hearts prevents the Lord hearing our prayers.

8. After we spend time with the Lord praying, reading God's Word, confessing our sin, and asking Him to fill us, are we automatically filled with the Spirit the entire day? Please explain your answer.
It is one thing to spend time with God in the morning, but we must "walk in the Spirit," meaning we must remain sensitive to His still small voice and follow Him throughout the day.

9. What are some ways we can remain sensitive to the Holy Spirit throughout our day?
Answers will vary but may include: meditating on a verse, avoiding temptation, holding our tongues, pausing to pray throughout the day.

10. In what areas of your life do you need the Holy Spirit's power? Will you seek His filling and power today?
Answers will vary.

Memory Verse

EPHESIANS 5:18
18 And be not drunk with wine, wherein is excess; but be filled with the Spirit;

LESSON FOUR

Generosity Makes a Difference

Key Verses

Acts 4:31–37

Lesson Theme

To make a difference, we must resist our selfish nature and cultivate generosity toward the Lord and others.

Lesson Overview

How did the early church respond when suddenly thousands of new believers found themselves in need? This lesson focuses our attention on the spirit of generosity that existed in the lives of these godly Christians.

First, we will examine the foundational Christian disciplines and perspectives that enabled the first-century church to become a generous people. Second, we will focus our attention on one particular illustration of generosity from which we can learn.

Teaching Outline

  I. The Perspective of Generosity
- A. An obligation toward others
- B. An openness toward ownership

 II. The Prerequisites for Generosity
- A. The discipline of prayer
- B. The disposition of grace

III. The Personality of Generosity
- A. A people who did not lack
- B. A man who sold his land

LESSON FOUR

Generosity Makes
a Difference

Text

Acts 4:31–37

Introduction

The first generation of Christians turned the world upside
down (Acts 17:6). How did they accomplish this feat? How
did they make a difference? So far we have learned that they
made a difference by investing in their relationships, caring
for the needs of others, and being filled with the Holy Spirit.

We left our study in verse 31, when those Christians
had gathered for prayer and received the fullness of the
Spirit. What did they do next? Where did they go from
there? Besides witnessing, which is an obvious result of
the fullness of the Holy Spirit, they gave. They dug deep,
and they began meeting the financial needs in their young

> *"The only antidote to materialism is giving, because it is exactly the opposite of greed."*
> —Ralph Doudera

congregation. Some sold land. Some sold houses. No doubt, others contributed in different ways.

Human nature leans toward materialism, selfishness, and greed. These Christians quickly squelched those temptations and rolled up their sleeves in a demonstration of generosity, and their generosity made a difference.

As we examine the lives of the Christians in Acts 4, we uncover **three lessons regarding Christian generosity.**

I. The Perspective of Generosity

ACTS 4:32

32 And the multitude of them that believed were of one heart and of one soul: neither said any of them that ought of the things which he possessed was his own; but they had all things common.

Generous Christians possess a unique perspective. They see things differently than others do. Consider the following two characteristics of the way generous people see things:

A. An obligation toward others

The Christians we read about in Acts 4:32 did not see themselves as independent from one another, but as interdependent on one another. They did not see things in terms of "us and them," or "mine and theirs," but in terms of "we and ours."

LESSON FOUR—GENEROSITY MAKES A DIFFERENCE

They considered another member's need as seriously as their own. They recognized the built-in obligation to one another that came with their relationship in Christ.

1 CORINTHIANS 12:12, 25–26
12   For as the body is one, and hath many members, and all the members of that one body, being many, are one body: so also is Christ.
25   That there should be no schism in the body; but that the members should have the same care one for another.
26   And whether one member suffer, all the members suffer with it; or one member be honoured, all the members rejoice with it.

The Apostle John expressed this obligation toward our fellow believers under the inspiration of the Holy Spirit.

1 JOHN 3:17
17   But whoso hath this world's good, and seeth his brother have need, and shutteth up his bowels of compassion from him, how dwelleth the love of God in him?

B. An openness toward ownership

Notice the telling expression found in the heart of verse 32, "*…neither said any of them that ought of the things which he possessed was his own….*" These people did not grasp their possessions with clenched fists. Instead, they had open hearts and open hands. They loosely held the things of this world. They knew that they could not serve God and mammon (Matthew 6:24), and they settled this matter quickly.

This description would not aptly fit some of us. We are more like the child in the nursery who, when he sees another child eyeing his toy or reaching for his snack,

51

quickly snatches the item and emphatically cries out, "Mine!" How sad that some people carry this disposition into adulthood.

Jesus said, *"freely ye have received, freely give"* (Matthew 10:8).

The Apostle Paul challenged us to have the right attitude in this area of life:

2 Corinthians 9:7

7 Every man according as he purposeth in his heart, so let him give; not grudgingly, or of necessity: for God loveth a cheerful giver.

Solomon knew something about accumulating wealth, yet he discouraged us from refusing to meet another's need. In fact, he said, that kind of thinking actually tends toward poverty.

Proverbs 11:24

24 There is that scattereth, and yet increaseth; and there is that withholdeth more than is meet, but it tendeth to poverty.

Illustration

In his book *Wealth Conundrum* Ralph Doudera, a highly successful investor, comments on the parable in Luke 12:18–21 about the rich man who was eager to build bigger barns. Doudera says, "Jesus teaches without reservation that there is a coming judgment on all those who hoard wealth for themselves. This man did not stop to think that perhaps the reason God made him affluent was so he could pass something on to the less fortunate."

Doudera then described a transition in his own spiritual walk when he realized that his investment firm

LESSON FOUR—GENEROSITY MAKES A DIFFERENCE

actually belonged to God, not him. He said he had a "dialogue" with God (nothing audible, just an attempt at describing how the Holy Spirit was working in his heart). It went like this:

"Lord, I am beginning to see what You are saying. Instead of You working for me, I should work for You? It will be Your business?"

"Yes, but you don't get the profits. They are Mine."

"Let me get this straight, You get the profits? What do You want with them?"

"There are lots of very important things that I would like to do, but the people who want to accomplish them do not have the funds. Even as we speak now, they are in tears petitioning Me for funds to do very urgent and necessary things."

"So You want my profits to be given to them?"

"No, I want MY profits to be given to them."

David had it right when he said to the Lord at the temple offering, *"...all things come of thee, and of thine own have we given thee"* (1 Chronicles 29:14). Everything we have already belongs to God.

II. The Prerequisites for Generosity

A couple of characteristics surface in the lives of the believers that preceded their acts of generosity. What enabled them to be generous?

A. *The discipline of prayer*

ACTS 4:31

31 And when they had prayed, the place was shaken where they were assembled together; and they were all

53

filled with the Holy Ghost, and they spake the word of God with boldness.

Some people will not become generous Christians until they become praying Christians. Prayer and generosity go hand-in-hand.

There seem to be two kinds of believers when it comes to the matters of prayer and generosity:

The first group is seen here in Acts 4. They are selfless, sacrificial, and sharing. And while they share with others, they seek the Lord for their own needs. They are sensitive to Him as He directs them to meet the needs of others.

The second group could not be more different. We learn of them in James 4. They are tight-fisted and discontented—they want more. They do not see God as their source of provision. The way they see it, "it's every man for himself," and they battle and claw to meet their own needs. Funny thing—these people never seem to have quite enough.

JAMES 4:1–2

1 From whence come wars and fightings among you? come they not hence, even of your lusts that war in your members?
2 Ye lust, and have not: ye kill, and desire to have, and cannot obtain: ye fight and war, yet ye have not, because ye ask not.

Will you be an *Acts 4 Christian* (praying and generous), or a *James 4 Christian* (prayerless and selfish)?

B. The disposition of grace

ACTS 4:33

33 And with great power gave the apostles witness of the resurrection of the Lord Jesus: and great grace was upon them all.

LESSON FOUR—GENEROSITY MAKES A DIFFERENCE

Grace, defined as "a disposition created by the Holy Spirit," enabled them to freely give.

Grace—God's work in our hearts—is what enables us to be generous. A generous Christian is one who has not forgotten how gracious God was in reaching down and saving his soul. Because he has received God's grace, he can share God's grace with others.

In the New Testament Epistles, generosity was often urged in the lives of Christians. When God wanted to encourage people to be generous, He often reminded them of the importance of grace. Let's look at Paul's classic passage on generosity. Or should we say, his passage on *grace?*

DEFINITION

Strong's *defines the Greek word* charis *(χάρις pronounced khar´-ece) as "...the divine influence upon the heart, and its reflection in the life."*

---

2 CORINTHIANS 8:1–9

1 Moreover, brethren, we do you to wit of the grace of God bestowed on the churches of Macedonia;

2 How that in a great trial of affliction the abundance of their joy and their deep poverty abounded unto the riches of their liberality.

3 For to their power, I bear record, yea, and beyond their power they were willing of themselves;

4 Praying us with much intreaty that we would receive the gift, and take upon us the fellowship of the ministering to the saints.

5 And this they did, not as we hoped, but first gave their own selves to the Lord, and unto us by the will of God.

6 Insomuch that we desired Titus, that as he had begun, so he would also finish in you the same grace also.

7 Therefore, as ye abound in every thing, in faith, and utterance, and knowledge, and in all diligence, and in your love to us, see that ye abound in this grace also.

8 I speak not by commandment, but by occasion of the forwardness of others, and to prove the sincerity of your love.

9 For ye know the grace of our Lord Jesus Christ, that, though he was rich, yet for your sakes he became poor, that ye through his poverty might be rich.

III. The Personality of Generosity

Toward the end of chapter 4, the focus shifts from the general description of the crowd and their needs to specific stories of faith, sacrifice, and provision.

A. A people who did not lack

ACTS 4:34–35

34 Neither was there any among them that lacked: for as many as were possessors of lands or houses sold them, and brought the prices of the things that were sold,

35 And laid them down at the apostles' feet: and distribution was made unto every man according as he had need.

First, notice that each person's individual need was met as people openly shared what God had given them. What a great scene! There was sufficiency because there was first generosity.

Lesson Four—Generosity Makes a Difference

Some people have a distorted view. They think that God wants their money and that He expects them to do without. They forget that this is the magnanimous God who spared not His own Son (Romans 8:32).

God is faithful and generous. But He wants us to surrender to Him and trust in Him—not in ourselves—to meet our needs. Jesus dealt with this issue in the Sermon on the Mount:

Matthew 6:26–32

26 Behold the fowls of the air: for they sow not, neither do they reap, nor gather into barns; yet your heavenly Father feedeth them. Are ye not much better than they?

27 Which of you by taking thought can add one cubit unto his stature?

28 And why take ye thought for raiment? Consider the lilies of the field, how they grow; they toil not, neither do they spin:

29 And yet I say unto you, That even Solomon in all his glory was not arrayed like one of these.

30 Wherefore, if God so clothe the grass of the field, which to day is, and to morrow is cast into the oven, shall he not much more clothe you, O ye of little faith?

31 Therefore take no thought, saying, What shall we eat? or, What shall we drink? or, Wherewithal shall we be clothed?

32 (For after all these things do the Gentiles seek:) for your heavenly Father knoweth that ye have need of all these things.

Paul also corrected this skewed mindset about God. God's plan is not deprivation, but sufficiency. God does not want giving to be an unbearable burden on a few, but an exercise of equal generosity and ample supply.

2 Corinthians 8:13–15

13 For I mean not that other men be eased, and ye burdened:

14 But by an equality, that now at this time your abundance may be a supply for their want, that their abundance also may be a supply for your want: that there may be equality:

15 As it is written, He that had gathered much had nothing over; and he that had gathered little had no lack.

B. A man who sold his land

Acts 4:36–37

36 And Joses, who by the apostles was surnamed Barnabas, (which is, being interpreted, The son of consolation,) a Levite, and of the country of Cyprus,

37 Having land, sold it, and brought the money, and laid it at the apostles' feet.

Barnabas will forever be remembered as a man who made a difference. Think about his simple decision to sell a vacant parcel of land and give the money to meet the congregation's needs.

He could have used this land for something self-serving. I suspect it was sitting idle since Barnabas stayed quite busy spreading the Gospel. What difference was that land making as it lay fallow? None whatsoever. But when he sold it, he was able to use the proceeds to make a difference. With what he received for that land, he was able to feed some otherwise hungry Christians, clothe some otherwise naked Christians, and put roofs over the heads of some otherwise homeless Christians.

Because of generosity, God used a dry, dusty patch of land to meet a need, and it serves today as an example to all Christians. That's the difference that generosity makes.

LESSON FOUR—GENEROSITY MAKES A DIFFERENCE

Jesus challenged His listeners to seize the "unrighteous mammon" of this world—referring to money—and to use it for the advancement of His kingdom and purposes (Luke 16:9–13).

Money has no eternal value until it is invested into an eternal work. One hundred dollars in my bank account has no significance beyond this world. But one hundred dollars given to a missionary for the purpose of printing Bibles or building a church will make a difference for eternity.

Generous people have learned that money can make a difference. Giving to meet the needs of the work of God or to meet the needs of others truly makes a difference.

- A few dollars that buys a gallon of gas for a bus makes a difference in the lives of children.

- A few hundred dollars that pays to print tracts makes a difference in the lives of those who receive them.

- A few thousand dollars used to purchase building materials and pay contractors makes a difference in the life of every person who sits under that new roof. It makes a difference each time the Scriptures are taught under that roof, each time a person is saved under that roof, and each time a child embraces the faith of his parents under that roof.

Don't squander your money on things that don't last. Invest as much of it as you can into what God values, and you will make a difference.

2 Corinthians 4:18

18 While we look not at the things which are seen, but at the things which are not seen: for the things which are seen are temporal; but the things which are not seen are eternal.

Colossians 3:2

2 Set your affection on things above, not on things on the earth.

Conclusion

Generosity not only makes a difference in the lives of others, it also makes a difference in our own lives.

Consider Barnabas: beyond Acts 4, we discover that he mentored Christians in Antioch, traveled with the Apostle Paul, and spread the Gospel to new regions as a missionary himself. But when did that lifestyle of faith and service begin?

It began when he learned to loosen his grip on the things of this world. Nudged by the Holy Spirit, he made a simple decision to sell a piece of vacant land. In essence, he learned to become a generous Christian, and generous Christians make a difference.

LESSON FOUR—GENEROSITY MAKES A DIFFERENCE

Study Questions

1. Generous Christians see things differently from those who are not generous. What are two characteristics of generous people?
    An obligation to others

    An openness toward others

2. What does 1 Corinthians 12:25–26 say about the body of Christ?
    Answers will vary. There are many members within that body, and when one suffers, all suffer with it. When a body part of the human body is injured, it affects the whole human body; so it is with the body of Christ.

3. What kind of giver does God love?
    God loves a cheerful giver.

4. Name the two prerequisites of generosity.
    The discipline of prayer

    The disposition of grace

5. As discussed in the lesson, what is the difference between an Acts 4 Christian and a James 4 Christian?
    An Acts 4 Christian is one who prays and is generous, and a James 4 Christian is prayerless and selfish.

6. What word can be defined as "a disposition created by the Holy Spirit"?
    Grace

7. How many times is the word *grace* mentioned in 2 Corinthians 8:1–9?
Grace is mentioned four times.

8. God promises to supply all our needs, including basic physical needs: food, clothing and shelter. In the Sermon on the Mount, what did Jesus use as examples of His provision?
The fowls of the air, lilies of the field, grass of the field

9. What was Joses' surname in Acts 4:36, and what does it mean?
Joses was surnamed Barnabas, which means the "son of consolation."

10. Does becoming a generous person make a difference in your life or just in the lives of others? Please explain.
Answers will vary. Becoming a generous person means you learn to hold the things of this world loosely, and you place a priority on heavenly things. When these happen, you are obeying Colossians 3:2, which says, "Set your affection on things above, not on things on the earth."

Memory Verse

2 CORINTHIANS 8:9

9 *For ye know the grace of our Lord Jesus Christ, that, though he was rich, yet for your sakes he became poor, that ye through his poverty might be rich.*

LESSON FIVE

Faithfulness Makes a Difference

Key Verses

Acts 5:16–42

Lesson Theme

To make a difference, we must remain faithful to the Lord and to His work in our lives.

Lesson Overview

Surprisingly, not everyone was pleased with the first-century Christians' efforts to make a difference. Many sick folks had been healed; those possessed by demons had been set free; thousands of lost and confused people had found peace through a relationship with Jesus Christ. But the local religious leaders did not appreciate the popularity of Christ's followers and their message.

When opposition and persecution came, the believers responded with Christ-honoring steadfastness that serves as an example for us today—faithfulness does indeed make a difference.

Teaching Outline

   I. The Circumstances They Endured
      A. They endured an unfair arrest.
      B. They endured unfounded accusations.
      C. They endured unfortunate abuse.

  II. The Companionship They Experienced
      A. Christ's intervention gave liberty.
      B. Christ's instructions gave responsibility.

 III. The Character They Exhibited
      A. They resisted being silenced.
      B. They rejoiced in suffering.
      C. They refused to stop.

LESSON FIVE

Faithfulness Makes a Difference

Text

Acts 5:16–42

Introduction:

Opposition came upon the efforts of this young congregation like a torrential flood. Would they endure, or would they fold under the pressure? This group stood firm and remained faithful. They had *started* making a difference, and faithfulness enabled them to *continue* making a difference.

- **Faithfulness is one of the great characteristics of our God.** First Corinthians 1:9 and 10:13 both simply say, *"God is faithful."*

- **God is searching for faithful ones.** Proverbs 20:6 tells us, *"Most men will proclaim every one his own goodness: but a faithful man who can find?"*

- **Faithfulness is a quality that God requires.** First Corinthians 4:2 states, *"Moreover it is required in stewards, that a man be found faithful."*

- **Special blessings are reserved for the faithful.** Proverbs 28:20 promises, *"A faithful man shall abound with blessings."* Jesus said, *"…be thou faithful unto death, and I will give thee a crown of life"* (Revelation 2:10).

If you want to make a difference and go the distance, you should examine Acts 5 closely. There you will find *three important ingredients of faithfulness.*

I.   The Circumstances They Endured

Faithfulness always requires endurance through difficult circumstances. Paul commended the believers in Thessalonica for their patience and endurance:

2 THESSALONIANS 1:4
4   So that we ourselves glory in you in the churches of God for your patience and faith in all your persecutions and tribulations that ye endure:

Paul urged Timothy to endure the difficulties that he would encounter as a young servant leader:

2 TIMOTHY 2:3
3   Thou therefore endure hardness, as a good soldier of Jesus Christ.

LESSON FIVE—FAITHFULNESS MAKES A DIFFERENCE

2 TIMOTHY 4:5

5   But watch thou in all things, endure afflictions, do the work of an evangelist, make full proof of thy ministry.

Some folks say, "I'd be faithful, but I can't since I have encountered such difficult circumstances." These poor souls don't realize that the call to faithfulness directly implies difficulty. We sometimes forget that Jesus said, *"In the world ye shall have tribulation…"* (John 16:33).

Consider a few of the difficult circumstances through which these believers remained faithful.

A. They endured an unfair arrest.

ACTS 5:17–18

17   *Then the high priest rose up, and all they that were with him, (which is the sect of the Sadducees,) and were filled with indignation,*
18   *And laid their hands on the apostles, and put them in the common prison.*

The apostles committed no crime, except preaching the Gospel of Christ, yet they were put into prison.

Commentary on Acts 5:17

As the religious "Supreme Court" of the Jewish people, the Sanhedrin routinely sat in judgment on new teachings and cult groups that sprang up. Their anger at the apostles was sharpened by the fact that Jesus had been crucified just a few weeks earlier, but His crucifixion had not stopped His doctrine and teaching from spreading among the people as they had hoped.—*Acts: The Church Alive*, by Paul Chappell

67

Some Christians become disheartened and even question God when they are treated unfairly. Life is unfair by nature. It wasn't fair that Jesus went to the Cross and bore our sins, but it was the will of God. God's purpose—not fairness—settles the circumstances of our lives. Jesus taught us to *expect* unfair treatment:

JOHN 15:20

20 *Remember the word that I said unto you, The servant is not greater than his lord. If they have persecuted me, they will also persecute you; if they have kept my saying, they will keep yours also.*

B. They endured unfounded accusations.

ACTS 5:27–28

27 *And when they had brought them, they set them before the council: and the high priest asked them,*

28 *Saying, Did not we straitly command you that ye should not teach in this name? and, behold, ye have filled Jerusalem with your doctrine, and intend to bring this man's blood upon us.*

Sometimes well-intentioned, sincere Christian servants are falsely accused—their motives questioned or their actions viewed with skepticism. This condemnation is painful, but it is to be expected as a follower of Christ.

LUKE 23:10

10 *And the chief priests and scribes stood and vehemently accused him.*

Throughout the ministry of the Apostle Paul, people literally fabricated accusations against him. Paul

LESSON FIVE—FAITHFULNESS MAKES A DIFFERENCE

responded to the Roman court, *"Neither can they prove the things whereof they now accuse me"* (Acts 24:13).

God's Word exposes the source of these accusations—Satan himself, *"the accuser of our brethren"* (Revelation 12:10).

> The most powerful way to answer your critics is to finish your task.

Peter encouraged us to maintain a clear conscience, even in the midst of unfounded accusations. In the end, the evil speakers will be ashamed if we remain faithful.

1 PETER 3:16

16 *Having a good conscience; that, whereas they speak evil of you, as of evildoers, they may be ashamed that falsely accuse your good conversation in Christ.*

C. They endured unfortunate abuse.

ACTS 5:40

40 *And to him they agreed: and when they had called the apostles, and beaten them, they commanded that they should not speak in the name of Jesus, and let them go.*

Jesus told His disciples that His kingdom's expansion and culmination would involve the physical mistreatment—even the martyrdom—of His choice servants:

MARK 13:9

9 *But take heed to yourselves: for they shall deliver you up to councils; and in the synagogues ye shall be beaten: and ye shall be brought before rulers and kings for my sake, for a testimony against them.*

Making a Difference

LUKE 21:16–17

16   And ye shall be betrayed both by parents, and brethren, and kinsfolks, and friends; and some of you shall they cause to be put to death.

17   And ye shall be hated of all men for my name's sake.

May those of us living in the twenty-first century respond properly to the freedoms we enjoy. First, may we be thankful. And second, may we take advantage of every opportunity to serve and witness for our Lord.

II. The Companionship They Experienced

ACTS 5:19–21

19   But the angel of the Lord by night opened the prison doors, and brought them forth, and said,

20   Go, stand and speak in the temple to the people all the words of this life.

21   And when they heard that, they entered into the temple early in the morning, and taught. But the high priest came, and they that were with him, and called the council together, and all the senate of the children of Israel, and sent to the prison to have them brought.

Notice what happened as a result of the companionship of the Lord Jesus Christ:

A. Christ's intervention gave liberty.

Just as for other men in Scripture (Daniel, Peter, Paul, and others), God physically sent His Angel to deliver His servants.

Lesson Five—Faithfulness Makes a Difference

Psalm 34:19

19   Many are the afflictions of the righteous: but the LORD delivereth him out of them all.

2 Timothy 3:11

11   Persecutions, afflictions, which came unto me at Antioch, at Iconium, at Lystra; what persecutions I endured: but out of them all the Lord delivered me.

We must never forget our Lord's promise attached to the Great Commission: *"…and, lo, I am with you alway…"* (Matthew 28:20).

That night, God set the apostles free from the prison in Jerusalem. And He is just as present—and just as willing—to accompany us through our seasons of difficulty. The psalmist tells us, *"God is our refuge and strength, a very present help in trouble"* (Psalm 46:1).

Paul recalled a similar moment in his life and ministry:

2 Timothy 4:16–18

16   At my first answer no man stood with me, but all men forsook me: I pray God that it may not be laid to their charge.

17   Notwithstanding the Lord stood with me, and strengthened me; that by me the preaching might be fully known, and that all the Gentiles might hear: and I was delivered out of the mouth of the lion.

18   And the Lord shall deliver me from every evil work, and will preserve me unto his heavenly kingdom: to whom be glory for ever and ever. Amen.

B. Christ's instructions gave responsibility.

ACTS 5:20

20 Go, stand and speak in the temple to the people all the words of this life.

God didn't free the apostles from prison so they could run and hide. He freed them so they could resume their ministry of teaching and preaching the Gospel.

When you were freed from sin, you received a great benefit, no doubt! But you weren't made free only for your benefit. You were set free so that you might speak for and serve the Lord who liberated you.

ROMANS 6:22A

22A But now being made free from sin, and become servants to God…

Even centuries before this day in Acts, God was in the business of setting His people free for the purpose of serving Him:

EXODUS 8:1

1 And the LORD spake unto Moses, Go unto Pharaoh, and say unto him, Thus saith the LORD, Let my people go, that they may serve me.

III. The Character They Exhibited

Considering the faithful nature of the apostles and first-century Christians, we observe three specific ways they exhibited their faithfulness:

LESSON FIVE—FAITHFULNESS MAKES A DIFFERENCE

A. They resisted being silenced.

ACTS 5:27–29

27 And when they had brought them, they set them before the council: and the high priest asked them,

28 Saying, Did not we straitly command you that ye should not teach in this name? and, behold, ye have filled Jerusalem with your doctrine, and intend to bring this man's blood upon us.

29 Then Peter and the other apostles answered and said, We ought to obey God rather than men.

This reminds us of a past situation when Peter and John said, possibly to the same group of religious leaders, "We cannot but speak the things which we have seen and heard" (Acts 4:20). They would not be silenced!

This scenario reveals God's perspective on matters of submission to authority. "Let every soul be subject unto the higher powers. For there is no power but of God: the powers that be are ordained of God" (Romans 13:1).

Peter encouraged Christians to submit to governmental authority, however ungodly they may be.

1 PETER 2:13–14

13 Submit yourselves to every ordinance of man for the Lord's sake: whether it be to the king, as supreme;

14 Or unto governors, as unto them that are sent by him for the punishment of evildoers, and for the praise of them that do well.

Whenever possible, we are taught to obey the authorities in our lives though obedience may be inconvenient, costly, or painful. However, when there arises a situation in which we must choose between obeying men and obeying God, we must choose God!

73

Our pastor has stated that if the day comes when he is limited in his freedom to preach particular truths from the Scriptures, he is still bound by God's Word to preach *"all the counsel of God"* (Acts 20:27). Similarly, if a new ordinance restricts us from witnessing on our streets, we should then respond as the apostles, "We ought to obey God, rather than men."

Don't let an intimidating coworker, a gruff neighbor, or even your own hesitant flesh, silence your witness for Christ.

B. They rejoiced in suffering.

ACTS 5:40–41

40 And to him they agreed: and when they had called the apostles, and beaten them, they commanded that they should not speak in the name of Jesus, and let them go.
41 And they departed from the presence of the council, rejoicing that they were counted worthy to suffer shame for his name.

This may be one of the most paradoxical passages in the Word of God. *"When they had called the apostles, and beaten them… they departed from the presence of the council, **rejoicing.**"*

Beaten…released…rejoicing?! It was not the suffering itself they enjoyed but the opportunity to identify with their Saviour who had done so much for them and to demonstrate their loyalty to Him.

1 PETER 4:12–13

12 Beloved, think it not strange concerning the fiery trial which is to try you, as though some strange thing happened unto you:

LESSON FIVE—FAITHFULNESS MAKES A DIFFERENCE

13 *But rejoice, inasmuch as ye are partakers of Christ's sufferings; that, when his glory shall be revealed, ye may be glad also with exceeding joy.*

Illustration

Polycarp (AD 70–155) was bishop of Smyrna and a godly man. He had known the Apostle John personally. When he was urged by the Roman proconsul to renounce Christ, Polycarp said: "Eighty and six years have I served Him, and He never did me any injury. How then can I blaspheme my King and my Saviour?" "I have respect for your age," said the official. "Simply say, 'Away with the atheists!' and be set free." The aged Polycarp pointed to the pagan crowd and said, "Away with the atheists!" He was burned at the stake and gave joyful testimony of his faith in Jesus Christ.—*Acts: The Church Alive*, by Paul Chappell

C. They refused to stop.

ACTS 5:42

42 *And daily in the temple, and in every house, they ceased not to teach and preach Jesus Christ.*

"*They ceased not*" reveals the faithful character of these Christians—character God has called us to emulate.

1 CORINTHIANS 15:58

58 *Therefore, my beloved brethren, be ye stedfast, unmoveable, always abounding in the work of the Lord, forasmuch as ye know that your labour is not in vain in the Lord.*

MAKING A DIFFERENCE

Illustration

The Bohemian reformer **John Huss** was a man who believed the Scriptures to be the infallible and supreme authority in all matters. He died at the stake in Constance, Germany, for that belief on his forty-second birthday. As he refused a final plea to renounce his faith, Huss's last words were, "What I taught with my lips, I seal with my blood."—*Acts: The Church Alive*, by Paul Chappell

Conclusion

If we do not remain faithful, our efforts to make a difference will be undone. When people speak of those who have impacted their lives, a common characteristic seems to surface—faithfulness.

"The test of your character is what it takes to stop you."
—Dr. Bob Jones, Sr.

Have you ever heard anyone say, "I stand grateful today for a mentor who used to serve the Lord, but in the end did not remain faithful"? Only when we are faithful, can we make a difference.

LESSON FIVE—FAITHFULNESS MAKES A DIFFERENCE

Study Questions

1. According to 1 Corinthians 4:2, what does God require of Christians?
    God requires faithfulness.

2. According to our lesson, what are three of the difficulties the first-century Christians endured?
    An unfair arrest
    Unfounded accusations
    Unfortunate abuse

3. Christians often expect their lives to go smoothly because they are Christians. But what does Jesus say to expect from the world? Use Scripture to support your answer.
    Persecution, hard times; John 15:20, 2 Thessalonians, 2 Timothy 4:5

4. Who is "the accuser" of the brethren?
    Satan

5. Explain how persecution and difficulty could be good for a Christian.
    Answers will vary. We are told in Psalm 46:1 that God is a very present help in trouble. When we are faced with difficulties, we should draw closer to God. Trials should not be the only time we are close to God, but they should cause us to seek His face more diligently.

6. What are some ways you can model faithfulness to your children and others?
    Faithfulness in Bible reading, prayer, church attendance, serving, loving your spouse, etc.

MAKING A DIFFERENCE

7. What are three ways the apostles exhibited their faithfulness?
They resisted being silenced.

They rejoiced in suffering.

They refused to stop.

8. Our world is becoming less tolerant to Christianity, and our freedom to speak God's truths could become limited. What verse tells us that we are to obey God rather than men?
Acts 5:29

9. First Peter 4:12–13 speaks of rejoicing as partakers of Christ's sufferings. How is it possible for someone to suffer and rejoice at the same time?
Answers will vary. A Christian would not rejoice because of the suffering itself; rather he would rejoice at the opportunity to demonstrate his faithfulness and loyalty to Jesus Christ—the one who suffered for him.

10. When people look at your life, do they see faithfulness? Is there an area in which you have been lacking faithfulness? Take a moment today to recommit to a life of faithfulness to the Lord.
Answers will vary.

Memory Verse

ACTS 5:42

42 And daily in the temple, and in every house, they ceased not to teach and preach Jesus Christ.

LESSON SIX

Teamwork Makes a Difference

Key Verses

Acts 6:1–7

Lesson Theme

To make a difference, we must work together to solve problems, to share responsibility, and to reach people for Christ.

Lesson Overview

The devil is constantly attempting to divide the followers of Christ. But God's Word emphasizes the importance of cultivating and maintaining unity.

PSALM 133:1

1 Behold, how good and how pleasant it is for brethren to dwell together in unity!

EPHESIANS 4:3

3 Endeavouring to keep the unity of the Spirit in the bond of peace.

This lesson focuses on the early church's response to a potentially divisive situation. Their solution involved the cooperative teamwork of godly, Spirit-filled men who assisted the apostles in serving the first-century Christians.

Teaching Outline

    I. Teamwork Produced a Decisive Remedy
- A. The reality of the need
- B. The responsibility of the believers
- C. The priority of the apostles
- D. The practicality of the solution

   II. Teamwork Produced Divided Responsibility
- A. A sincere work—"of honest report"
- B. A spiritual walk—"full of the Holy Ghost"
- C. A sensible wisdom—"and wisdom, whom we may appoint over this business"

  III. Teamwork Produced Divine Results
- A. Their need was met.
- B. Their number was multiplied.
- C. Their nation was moved.

LESSON SIX

Teamwork Makes
a Difference

Text

Acts 6:1–7

Introduction

Throughout the first five chapters of Acts, the early church was truly making a difference. They were working on their relationships, caring for others, experiencing the fullness of the Spirit, exercising generosity toward those in need, and remaining faithful in the face of opposition.

By the time we arrive at chapter 6, this congregation had grown to many thousands of people, and their Gospel impact was expanding. But now they would deal with a new challenge—a challenge from within. A problem had surfaced in the church, and how the Christians dealt with it could very well determine the future success of their movement.

81

We will briefly look at the details of their problem. But we will focus our attention mostly on their solution, which was to set apart seven new servant leaders in the church.

> *"Much of the work of God is carried on by unknown, unsung individuals who faithfully carry out the tasks entrusted to them, quite content to leave the limelight to others."*
> —John Phillips

Today, as then, we need teamwork among God's people. We need men and women of different backgrounds and upbringings, working together in harmony.

Of the seven who were chosen, we know Stephen as the first martyr. We remember that Philip (not the Apostle) was the church's first missionary. We know very little about Prochorus, and we know nothing else of the remaining four: Nicanor, Timon, Parmenas, and Nicolas.

We discover from the early church's development of life and ministry *three products of biblical teamwork.*

I. Teamwork Produced a Decisive Remedy

Until natural friction develops, there's no real test of a team's strength. This group of Christians saw the need that surfaced as an opportunity to draw them closer, not as a wedge to drive them apart.

A. The reality of the need

Verse 1 tells us about the need: "*there arose a murmuring of the Grecians against the Hebrews, because their widows were neglected in the daily ministration.*"

LESSON SIX—TEAMWORK MAKES A DIFFERENCE

There were two Jewish sub-groups in the Jerusalem congregation. First, there were the more traditional, strict *Hebrew* Jews. Second, there were the more progressive, Greek-influenced *Hellenist* Jews. As the needs of the poor, specifically the widows, were met in this congregation, the Hellenist Jews questioned the fairness of the distribution of resources. They felt that the Hebrew Jews, who were in charge of delivering the charity, were discriminating against their widows.

> God is not nearly as concerned about assigning the blame as He is about solving the problem.

We are not told whether this was a legitimate grievance, or just a product of the Hellenists' perception. But one thing was clear: the apostles were not going to allow the murmuring to continue without addressing it. Interestingly, there was no significant debate over where the fault lay. Either way, the problem needed to be solved.

Murmuring and complaining are never God's preferred responses to personal problems.

NUMBERS 11:1A

1A And when the people complained, it displeased the LORD:

The word *murmur* and its forms appear forty times in the Bible, and (would you believe it?) not one of those times is this activity mentioned in a positive context.

Moses told the ungrateful Jews, after their deliverance from Egypt, "...*the LORD heareth your murmurings which ye murmur against him: and what are we? your murmurings are not against us, but against the LORD*" (Exodus 16:8B).

83

PHILIPPIANS 2:14

14 Do all things without murmurings and disputings:

JUDE 16A

16A These are murmurers, complainers, walking after their own lusts;

B. The responsibility of the believers

When problems arise (and they will) what is our responsibility? It's not to complain or murmur but to take the problem to those who are part of the solution.

Notice that verse 2 says that the Apostles *"called the multitude of the disciples unto them."*

They had served the Lord together. They had suffered for Christ together. And now, they would solve a problem together.

There are two significant lessons to remember when studying this scene in the first-century congregation:

- As long as there are human beings in the church, there will be problems.

- As long as there are Spirit-filled leaders and members in the church, there will be solutions.

Problems will arise—there's no question. But when humble people come to honest leaders with a genuine need, a solution is sure to be near.

Our pastor has often said that spiritual Christians are able to make potentially large problems smaller, while carnal Christians tend to make small problems larger.

When there is a grievance between believers, the Lord Jesus taught us to make the situation right, with utmost urgency.

LESSON SIX—TEAMWORK MAKES A DIFFERENCE

MATTHEW 5:23–24

23 *Therefore if thou bring thy gift to the altar, and there rememberest that thy brother hath ought against thee;*
24 *Leave there thy gift before the altar, and go thy way; first be reconciled to thy brother, and then come and offer thy gift.*

In Matthew 18:15–17, Jesus explained to His followers their responsibility—not to run and hide or to whisper in the corner about difficult situations, but to *"go and tell him his fault."*

C. The priority of the apostles

Verse 4 explains the heart of the leaders: *"But we will give ourselves continually to prayer, and to the ministry of the word."*

The Apostles did not consider the task of managing the widows' benefits beneath them. They simply came to a common-sense conclusion. There was no point in leaving their core calling for a task that others were equally willing and able to accomplish.

All men and women in the church should pray. And many in the church share in ministering the Word. But certain God-called men among the assembly had obviously been set aside to give their lives to the sound teaching and preaching of doctrine. If the early church was to be firmly grounded in their new faith, they would need capable and dedicated students of the Word, who would be *"able to teach others also"* (2 Timothy 2:2).

Paul seemed to indicate that this was the special calling on Timothy's life, as well as his own:

1 Timothy 4:13–16

13   Till I come, give attendance to reading, to exhortation, to doctrine.

14   Neglect not the gift that is in thee, which was given thee by prophecy, with the laying on of the hands of the presbytery.

15   Meditate upon these things; give thyself wholly to them; that thy profiting may appear to all.

16   Take heed unto thyself, and unto the doctrine; continue in them: for in doing this thou shalt both save thyself, and them that hear thee.

1 Timothy 5:17

17   Let the elders that rule well be counted worthy of double honour, especially they who labour in the word and doctrine.

May we be thankful and appreciative toward those called ones who have dedicated their lives to diligently laboring in the Word and doctrine!

D. The practicality of the solution

The Apostles articulated a sensible, workable solution to meet the needs of all widows: *"look ye out among you seven men…whom we may appoint over this business"* (Acts 6:3).

The solution was as simple as finding other godly, gifted men who could look after responsibilities within the church. Peter tells us that *every* person should be involved in ministry.

1 Peter 4:10

10   As every man hath received the gift, even so minister the same one to another, as good stewards of the manifold grace of God.

The congregation gave this solution unanimous approval: *"And the saying pleased the whole multitude:"*

II. Teamwork Produced Divided Responsibility

Dividing the responsibilities within the local congregation wasn't just a good solution to a particular problem; it was and is God's plan for every local church. God has prepared and equipped each of His children to carry out a unique role and function within His body.

ROMANS 12:4–8

4   For as we have many members in one body, and all members have not the same office:

5   So we, being many, are one body in Christ, and every one members one of another.

6   Having then gifts differing according to the grace that is given to us, whether prophecy, let us prophesy according to the proportion of faith;

7   Or ministry, let us wait on our ministering: or he that teacheth, on teaching;

8   Or he that exhorteth, on exhortation: he that giveth, let him do it with simplicity; he that ruleth, with diligence; he that sheweth mercy, with cheerfulness.

1 CORINTHIANS 12:4–6

4   Now there are diversities of gifts, but the same Spirit.

5   And there are differences of administrations, but the same Lord.

6   And there are diversities of operations, but it is the same God which worketh all in all.

Each of us must realize that it is God's plan for us to accept and carry responsibility within the church. Are you ready to be entrusted with ministry responsibility? Can the congregation depend on you? Ignoring our responsibility and allowing others to carry the weight without our help is not an option found in the New Testament.

Take a note of three specific characteristics that qualify us to receive responsibility:

A. A sincere work—"of honest report"

These were to be genuine men, not hypocrites—men who did not merely "talk the talk" but also "walked the walk." They were to be godly men known for their integrity and genuine sincerity.

1 TIMOTHY 4:12

12 Let no man despise thy youth; but be thou an example of the believers, in word, in conversation, in charity, in spirit, in faith, in purity.

A *good report* was the last qualification that Paul listed for the office of the pastor:

1 TIMOTHY 3:7

7 Moreover he must have a good report of them which are without; lest he fall into reproach and the snare of the devil.

We know very little about the first-century Christian Demetrius. But the little John wrote of him speaks volumes.

3 JOHN 12A

12A Demetrius hath good report of all men,

LESSON SIX—TEAMWORK MAKES A DIFFERENCE

B. A spiritual walk—"full of the Holy Ghost"

These men were to be Holy Spirit-filled, under His control. As we learned from Acts 4, the fullness of the Spirit is found when one connects with God daily through Bible reading and prayer, cleanses his heart from sin, and then yields his life to the Spirit's control.

A Spirit-filled man is one whose temper is controlled, whose words are measured, whose thought life is pure, whose motives are noble, and whose walk is steady. He is not simply doing *his best* to get by. He is receiving a divine enabling to be a better man than he could have ever been on his own. He is demonstrating characteristics consistent with the Spirit who lives within.

GALATIANS 5:22–25

22 *But the fruit of the Spirit is love, joy, peace, longsuffering, gentleness, goodness, faith,*

23 *Meekness, temperance: against such there is no law.*

24 *And they that are Christ's have crucified the flesh with the affections and lusts.*

25 *If we live in the Spirit, let us also walk in the Spirit.*

C. A sensible wisdom—"and wisdom, whom we may appoint over this business"

These were to be wise and prudent men who were levelheaded and competent in God's ways and in His Word. The work of the church was too important to rely on those who would "wing it" or "shoot from the hip."

PROVERBS 4:5–7

5 *Get wisdom, get understanding: forget it not; neither decline from the words of my mouth.*

6 Forsake her not, and she shall preserve thee: love her, and she shall keep thee.
7 Wisdom is the principal thing; therefore get wisdom: and with all thy getting get understanding.

The measurement for godly wisdom is this: does one fear God? Some folks have business sense, book knowledge, or street smarts, but they do not fear God, and therefore do not qualify for His wisdom. According to Solomon, fearing God is where wisdom is born, and knowing Him is where wisdom is developed.

PROVERBS 9:10
10 The fear of the LORD is the beginning of wisdom: and the knowledge of the holy is understanding.

Moses, as he divided the responsibilities of God's work, was instructed to find this kind of man:

EXODUS 28:3
3 And thou shalt speak unto all that are wise hearted, whom I have filled with the spirit of wisdom, that they may make Aaron's garments to consecrate him, that he may minister unto me in the priest's office.

Joshua was also this kind of man.

DEUTERONOMY 34:9A
9A And Joshua the son of Nun was full of the spirit of wisdom;

III. Teamwork Produced Divine Results

Notice what happened as this story of teamwork unfolded.

Lesson Six—Teamwork Makes a Difference

A. Their need was met.

Apparently, the Hellenist Jews were satisfied with the new arrangement, because we never again hear a hint of difficulty in this department.

When God's people work together for solutions, in a humble, creative, biblical, servant-hearted fashion, He honors their efforts. Needs are met, remedies are found, and the work of God is able to march forward with new effectiveness and momentum.

Matthew 6:33

33 But seek ye first the kingdom of God, and his righteousness; and all these things shall be added unto you.

B. Their number was multiplied.

A noteworthy progression occurs in the language used to describe the church's growth in the book of Acts. Early in the book, Luke was given the word *added* to describe the growth of the congregation (Acts 2:41, 47; 5:14). However, here in chapter 6, the word *multiplied* is used for the first time (6:1, 7; 12:24).

This is the power of teamwork. When the first generation of disciples won folks to Christ, the church experienced *additions*. But when those converts told others, the church experienced *multiplication*.

This is what the Apostle Paul had in mind for Timothy's ministry in Ephesus:

2 Timothy 2:2

2 And the things that thou hast heard of me among many witnesses, the same commit thou to faithful men, who shall be able to teach others also.

C. Their nation was moved.

Verse 7 tells us, *"a great company of the priests were obedient to the faith."*

Commentary on Acts 6:7

And no wonder [they were saved]. They, more than anyone else, knew that the old-fashioned Judaism, of which they were the most visible and venerable representatives, was finished. There had been a day, not long before, when some of them had gone into the temple as usual to trim the lamps in the Holy Place, and they had been stopped cold in their tracks. The temple veil had been rent in two—from top to bottom! No human hand had done that.

For the first time the priests could look beyond the golden altar into the holiest of all and see the sacred Ark with the outspread wings of the cherubim. They could see where, generation after generation, the high priest on the Day of Atonement had sprinkled the blood. They had stood and stared.

The priests compared notes. The rending of the veil had happened the very moment Jesus of Nazareth had died. For a while they resisted the irrefutable evidence of the collapse of Judaism, but now a great company of them became obedient to the new faith.—*Exploring Acts,* by John Phillips, Loizeaux 1986

How pleased the Lord was with the salvation of these Jewish leaders. Both Jesus and the Apostles went *first* to the Jews with the message of the Gospel (Romans 1:16). God has always loved this special people and continues

Lesson Six—Teamwork Makes a Difference

to love them today. We are instructed to pray for their peace (Psalm 122:6) and to bless them (Genesis 12:3). The Apostle Paul expressed the heart of God for Israel, as well as his own heart for the salvation of his brethren:

ROMANS 10:1

1   Brethren, my heart's desire and prayer to God for Israel is, that they might be saved.

Conclusion

Our pastor often says, "Teamwork makes the dream work." Teamwork was common practice for the early church. They didn't waste energy assigning blame or comparing responsibilities. They each put their hands to the work, sharing the responsibility as the Lord saw fit. They each carried their weight on the team, making a difference for one another and to their part of the world for the cause of Christ. Will you?

Study Questions

1. In verse one of our text, who was being neglected?
   The widows

2. Did the apostles think they were "too good" to help with the present need? Why or why not?
   No, they did not think they were too good. Rather, they were doing what God had called them to do (prayer and the ministry of the Word), and they didn't want to leave their calling to do something that others could do.

3. When looking for someone to help with the needs in the church, the apostles required what three characteristics in the chosen men?
   Men of honest report, full of the Holy Ghost, full of wisdom

4. According to Psalm 133:1 and Ephesians 4:3, what is a vital ingredient for teamwork to happen?
   Unity

5. What is God more concerned about than ascribing blame?
   Solving the problem.

6. When problems arise between believers, what does Matthew 5:23–24 instruct us to do before bringing our gift to the altar?
   Leave our gift, go, and get things right with our brother.

Lesson Six—Teamwork Makes a Difference

7. Name the spiritual gifts listed in Romans 12.
   Prophecy, ministering, teaching, exhortation, giving, ruling, mercy

8. List the fruit of the Spirit in Galatians 5:22–23.
   Love, joy, peace, longsuffering, gentleness, goodness, faith, meekness, temperance

9. According to Proverbs 4:7, what is the most important thing?
   Wisdom

10. What were the results of teamwork given in our lesson?
    Their need was met.

    Their number was multiplied.

    Their nation was moved.

11. What are some practical ways you can be a team player?
    Answers will vary.

Memory Verses

GALATIANS 5:22–23
22 But the fruit of the Spirit is love, joy, peace, longsuffering, gentleness, goodness, faith,
23 Meekness, temperance: against such there is no law.

LESSON SEVEN

A Witness Makes a Difference

Key Verses

Acts 6:8–7:60

Lesson Theme

To make a difference, we must seek to be used as bold and clear witnesses for the Lord Jesus Christ.

Lesson Overview

In the previous lesson, we learned that teamwork enabled the first-century Christians in Jerusalem to make a difference. In this lesson, we'll narrow our focus to one member of that team. Stephen, the first martyr, was willing to lay down his life to make a difference as a witness for the Lord Jesus Christ. We can learn from his godly character, clear witness, and willingness to suffer at the hands of those who refused his message.

Teaching Outline

I. The Character of the Man
   A. Full of faith
   B. Full of power
   C. Irresistible wisdom
   D. Irresistible spirit

II. The Contradiction of the Mob
   A. The false accusers
   B. The face of an angel

III. The Content of the Message
   A. The review of their history
   B. The exposure of their hypocrisy
   C. The conviction of their hearts

IV. The Climax of the Meeting
   A. The Saviour stood.
   B. The scoffers stoned him.
   C. Saul studied him.
   D. Stephen suffered.
      1. With a Christ-like declaration
      2. With a forgiving disposition
      3. With a peaceful departure

LESSON SEVEN

A Witness Makes
a Difference

Text

Acts 6:8–7:60

Introduction

Following His resurrection, the Lord Jesus Christ met with
His disciples a number of times over a forty-day period before
His ascension back to Heaven (Acts 1:3). Notice that on two
of those occasions He used the term *witness* to describe the
future role of His disciples.

LUKE 24:46–48

*46 And said unto them, Thus it is written, and thus it behoved
Christ to suffer, and to rise from the dead the third day:*
*47 And that repentance and remission of sins should be preached
in his name among all nations, beginning at Jerusalem.*
48 And ye are witnesses of these things.

99

MAKING A DIFFERENCE

ACTS 1:8

8 But ye shall receive power, after that the Holy Ghost is come upon you: and ye shall be witnesses unto me both in Jerusalem, and in all Judaea, and in Samaria, and unto the uttermost part of the earth.

DEFINITION

Wiktionary *defines the term* witness *in the following manner:*
1. *Attestation of a fact or event*
2. *One who has a personal knowledge of something*
3. *Someone called to give evidence in a court*

This definition fits our use of the term *witness* since:

- We have been called to attest to the facts of our Lord's sacrifice on the Cross, His victory over death, and His willingness to save.

- Those of us who have been saved have personal knowledge of Christ's saving power.

- Our lives are intended to bear evidence of our relationship with Christ in the courtroom of everyday life.

We can learn **three lessons from the witness of Stephen.**

I.   The Character of the Man (vv. 6:8–10)

Underneath our witness must lie the foundation of a Christ-like character. Verses 8 and 10 outline four specific traits of Stephen's character.

Lesson Seven—A Witness Makes a Difference

A. Full of faith

ACTS 6:8

8 And Stephen, full of faith and power, did great wonders and miracles among the people.

People who lack faith conclude that God could not (or would not) use them as witnesses. Or they believe that even if He could, people would not listen. On the other hand, a person of faith says, "God *can* use me, and some people will listen!" The level of confidence you have in God determines how likely you are to witness for Him.

HEBREWS 11:6

6 But without faith it is impossible to please him: for he that cometh to God must believe that he is, and that he is a rewarder of them that diligently seek him.

Some Christians don't witness because they lack confidence in their own knowledge or skill. But true Christian witnessing begins, not with confidence in self, but with confidence in God. In fact, self-confident Christians find their efforts unproductive because their confidence in self will eliminate their dependence on God.

Paul told the church at Philippi that we are to *"have no confidence in the flesh"* (Philippians 3:3).

B. Full of power

Similarly, some wonder whether they possess the power to convince people of the Gospel. Again, our power comes from the Lord.

2 CORINTHIANS 4:7

7 But we have this treasure in earthen vessels, that the excellency of the power may be of God, and not of us.

Paul described the Christian life as an arrangement where God's presence—*"this treasure"*—is contained in imperfect people—*"earthen vessels."* If we yield to the Holy Spirit, we accomplish what God can do through us, not what we can do in our own best efforts (which is far less).

Our power is found in the Spirit of God *present in* us and the Word of God *presented by* us (Romans 10:17).

ZECHARIAH 4:6B

6B ...*Not by might, nor by power, but by my spirit, saith the* LORD *of hosts.* (also see Psalm 20:7)

C. Irresistible wisdom

ACTS 6:9–10

9 *Then there arose certain of the synagogue, which is called the synagogue of the Libertines, and Cyrenians, and Alexandrians, and of them of Cilicia and of Asia, disputing with Stephen.*

10 *And they were not able to resist the wisdom and the spirit by which he spake.*

A debate was heating up between this Hebrew Christian Stephen and his fellow Jews who still embraced their old system of worship. They were not pleased to hear that Jesus, whom they had crucified, was the very Messiah promised by the Old Testament prophets.

Apparently, Stephen was so well versed in the Scriptures and presented his arguments with such impelling reason that the Jews were speechless. Synagogue leaders were silenced and flustered in his presence. The case for Jesus Christ, made by the prophets and fulfilled in His incarnation, was flawless.

LESSON SEVEN—A WITNESS MAKES A DIFFERENCE

The synagogue referenced was likely the one where young Saul (eventually the Apostle Paul) studied and worshipped.

ACTS 22:3

3 I am verily a man which am a Jew, born in Tarsus, **a city in Cilicia**, yet brought up in this city at the feet of Gamaliel, and taught according to the perfect manner of the law of the fathers, and was zealous toward God, as ye all are this day.

HISTORICAL NOTE

Synagogues came into use during the Old Testament era when the Jews were scattered from their homeland, and could not worship at the temple. At these meeting places, the Scriptures were publicly read and taught to Jewish families. Most cities where a significant population of Jews resided eventually saw one or more synagogues constructed during this six hundred year period.

D. Irresistible spirit

Witnessing for Christ in the midst of an increasingly secular and hostile culture requires both godly wisdom and an excellent spirit. The word *spirit* is often used in the Scriptures to describe our attitudes or dispositions.

PROVERBS 17:27B

27B ...a man of understanding is of an excellent spirit.

Joseph and Daniel are both examples of men who had great attitudes and were able to make a difference in the lives of people whose culture countered their faith.

103

MAKING A DIFFERENCE

DANIEL 6:3

3 Then this Daniel was preferred above the presidents and princes, because an excellent spirit was in him; and the king thought to set him over the whole realm.

"It is not your aptitude, but your attitude, that determines your altitude."

—Curtis Hutson

As you witness to folks at work, in your neighborhood, and on the streets, demonstrate a great attitude. Ask God to enable you to exude the joy and enthusiasm that evidence a relationship with Him. As the children's song says, "If you're saved and you know it, then your life will surely show it!"

II. The Contradiction of the Mob (vv. 6:11–15)

As was the case with other Christian witnesses, such as Peter and James, not all present were glad to hear the good news of the Gospel.

A. The false accusers

ACTS 6:11–14

11 Then they suborned men, which said, We have heard him speak blasphemous words against Moses, and against God.

12 And they stirred up the people, and the elders, and the scribes, and came upon him, and caught him, and brought him to the council,

13 And set up false witnesses, which said, This man ceaseth not to speak blasphemous words against this holy place, and the law:

LESSON SEVEN—A WITNESS MAKES A DIFFERENCE

14 For we have heard him say, that this Jesus of Nazareth shall destroy this place, and shall change the customs which Moses delivered us.

The hypocrisy that existed in the lives of these committed Jews was quite a paradox. They were enraged over Stephen's apparent disregard for the law, but they dealt with this by breaking one of its most basic commands: "Thou shalt not bear false witness…" (Exodus 20:16).

FALSE ACCUSATIONS IN THE BIBLE

Like others in the Bible, Stephen was convicted by the testimony of false accusers.

- Jezebel hired false witnesses against Naboth in 1 Kings 21:9–13.
- The chief priests and elders solicited false witnesses against Jesus in Matthew 26:59–60.
- Paul faced the problem of false witnesses (Acts 24:13).

One of the main concerns of Stephen's accusers was that their customs remain intact (v. 14). While some traditions may prove helpful, human nature sometimes prefers religious or cultural customs over the truth of God's Word.

MARK 7:9
9 And he said unto them, Full well ye reject the commandment of God, that ye may keep your own tradition.

May God use us as He used Stephen to witness to those trapped in empty rituals, ceremonies, and traditions.

B. The face of an angel

ACTS 6:15

15 And all that sat in the council, looking stedfastly on him, saw his face as it had been the face of an angel.

Somehow Stephen was able to respond to their anger, violence, and accusations with grace. He did not recoil in fear. He did not retaliate in vengeance. His reply was a gracious countenance. We can demonstrate this kind of countenance only when we have spent time with God. Consider Moses upon his return from Mount Sinai:

EXODUS 34:30

30 And when Aaron and all the children of Israel saw Moses, behold, the skin of his face shone; and they were afraid to come nigh him.

Stephen responded to their threatening just as the Lord Jesus had responded several weeks prior. Notice how Peter described our Saviour's response.

1 PETER 2:23

23 Who, when he was reviled, reviled not again; when he suffered, he threatened not; but committed himself to him that judgeth righteously:

III. The Content of the Message (vv. 7:1–54)

Stephen defended His position as a follower of Christ. His message was filled with Scripture, and he built an airtight case for Jesus as the Messiah.

LESSON SEVEN—A WITNESS MAKES A DIFFERENCE

A. *The review of their history*

1. The faith of Abraham (vv. 2–8)

2. The trials of Joseph (vv. 9–17)

3. The bondage in Egypt (vv. 18–19)

4. The deliverance by Moses (vv. 20–36)

5. The disobedience of the Jews (vv. 37–43)

6. The purpose of the tabernacle and temple (vv. 44–50)

Stephen wisely drew attention to lessons from the Jews' history.

- Abraham followed in faith without the presence of a temple.

- Joseph, like Jesus (and now Stephen), was rejected by his brethren.

- The people rebelled against Moses and the prophets in favor of idolatry.

- A relationship with God was not based on a building.

His message was similar to the one that Jesus delivered to the woman at the well.

JOHN 4:23

23 But the hour cometh, and now is, when the true worshippers shall worship the Father in spirit and in truth: for the Father seeketh such to worship him.

B. The exposure of their hypocrisy

ACTS 7:51–53

51 Ye stiffnecked and uncircumcised in heart and ears, ye do always resist the Holy Ghost: as your fathers did, so do ye.
52 Which of the prophets have not your fathers persecuted? and they have slain them which shewed before of the coming of the Just One; of whom ye have been now the betrayers and murderers:
53 Who have received the law by the disposition of angels, and have not kept it.

Next, Stephen turned His message from their *history* to their *hypocrisy*. Even while they accused him, Stephen did not hesitate to point out their own guilt.

Commentary on Acts 7:51–53

They had accused him of reviling the Holy Place— he accused them of resisting the Holy Ghost.

They had accused him of slighting Moses, the man of God—he accused them of slaying Jesus, the Messiah of God.

They had accused him of blaspheming the law—he accused them of breaking the law.

—*Exploring Acts,* by John Phillips, Loizeaux 1986

When we witness, we must, in love, expose the guilt of the sinner. We cannot sugarcoat the fact that he stands guilty and condemned before God. In fact, until a sinner realizes his guilt, he will see no reason to turn to Christ. If he's not guilty, then he doesn't need the forgiveness Christ offers.

LESSON SEVEN—A WITNESS MAKES A DIFFERENCE

This is one key function of the law—to expose guilt and the resulting need for Christ.

ROMANS 3:19

19 Now we know that what things soever the law saith, it saith to them who are under the law: that every mouth may be stopped, and all the world may become guilty before God.

C. The conviction of their hearts

ACTS 7:54

54 When they heard these things, they were cut to the heart, and they gnashed on him with their teeth.

Without conviction there cannot be conversion. Unfortunately, most in this mob (not all, we will see) were convicted but not converted. None of them were converted that day, to our knowledge. Some resembled King Agrippa who, in spite of conviction, stiffened in his resistance to the Gospel.

ACTS 26:28

28 Then Agrippa said unto Paul, Almost thou persuadest me to be a Christian.

IV. The Climax of the Meeting (vv. 7:55–60)

This story began with a debate in the synagogue. Then it moved to a public square where the accusations were angrily hurled at Stephen. Now he has given his scriptural defense for his faith and has turned the crowd's attention to their own guilt. The suspense in this story could not have been greater, and its conclusion could not have been more dramatic.

109

A. The Saviour stood.

ACTS 7:55–56

55 But he, being full of the Holy Ghost, looked up stedfastly into heaven, and saw the glory of God, and Jesus standing on the right hand of God,

56 And said, Behold, I see the heavens opened, and the Son of man standing on the right hand of God.

In just a few minutes, Stephen would join His Lord in Heaven (2 Corinthians 5:8). But for this moment, the Saviour demonstrated His recognition of Stephen's suffering.

In Matthew 28:20, Jesus promised His presence for those who would witness for Him, "…and, lo, I am with you alway, even unto the end of the world." He takes note of His children's testimonies for Him.

HEBREWS 6:10

10 For God is not unrighteous to forget your work and labour of love, which ye have shewed toward his name, in that ye have ministered to the saints, and do minister.

When we make sacrifices for Christ or stand and speak up for Him in boldness and clarity, some may not notice, but Christ always notices.

B. The scoffers stoned him.

ACTS 7:57–58A

57 Then they cried out with a loud voice, and stopped their ears, and ran upon him with one accord,

58A And cast him out of the city, and stoned him:

They had endured enough of this witness. With a child's immaturity, they stuck their fingers in their ears, but with the power of an adult, they determined to kill him in outrage.

People who reject Jesus Christ do not reject Him because of *reason*. They do so because of a *refusal* to hear His Word.

JEREMIAH 29:19

19 Because they have not hearkened to my words, saith the LORD, which I sent unto them by my servants the prophets, rising up early and sending them; but ye would not hear, saith the LORD.

C. Saul studied him.

ACTS 7:58B

58B …and the witnesses laid down their clothes at a young man's feet, whose name was Saul.

A young man, who just two short chapters later would be saved, was near the place of Stephen's stoning, cheering on the mob. The testimony of a gracious, witnessing martyr made an indelible impact on young Saul. In fact, when his turn came to witness for the Lord Jesus, he recalled this scene:

ACTS 22:20

20 And when the blood of thy martyr Stephen was shed, I also was standing by, and consenting unto his death, and kept the raiment of them that slew him.

No doubt, some in the early church considered Stephen's stoning a needless tragedy. However, we cannot always measure the scope of our witness for Christ. Some who do not see a large harvest in their own personal ministries may have an impact beyond their knowledge.

Illustration

Professor Howard Hendricks tells about an eighty-three-year-old Michigan woman he met at a Sunday school training seminar he was conducting in Chicago. In a church with a Sunday school of only sixty-five people, she taught a class of thirteen boys. She had traveled by bus all the way to Chicago the night before the meeting, in her words, "to learn something that would make me a better teacher." Hendricks commented, "I thought at the time, most people who had a class of thirteen boys in a Sunday school of only sixty-five would be breaking their arms to pat themselves on the back. Not this lady." Hendricks went on to explain, "Eighty-four boys who sat under her teaching are now in full-time ministry. Twenty-two are graduates of the seminary where I teach.—*Teaching to Change Lives*, by Howard Hendricks

D. Stephen suffered.

ACTS 7:59–60

59 And they stoned Stephen, calling upon God, and saying, Lord Jesus, receive my spirit.

60 And he kneeled down, and cried with a loud voice, Lord, lay not this sin to their charge. And when he had said this, he fell asleep.

1. With a Christ-like declaration

Stephen committed his spirit into the Lord's care, just as Jesus had done.

LUKE 23:46

46 And when Jesus had cried with a loud voice, he said, Father, into thy hands I commend my spirit: and having said thus, he gave up the ghost.

2. With a forgiving disposition

Stephen followed Christ's example (Luke 23:34) as well as His instructions.

MATTHEW 5:44B

44B ...pray for them which despitefully use you, and persecute you;

3. With a peaceful departure

In a manner inconsistent with the violence occurring around him, Stephen closed his eyes in sleep. He was not dead, but alive on the other side with Christ, leaving his beaten body behind.

1 THESSALONIANS 4:13

13 But I would not have you to be ignorant, brethren, concerning them which are asleep, that ye sorrow not, even as others which have no hope.

Conclusion

Our theme for this series of lessons is *making a difference*. There are many ways we can make a difference. But perhaps none of those ways are as close to the heart of God as this one: being a witness to this world of His love and saving power.

LUKE 19:10

10 For the Son of man is come to seek and to save that which was lost.

Study Questions

1. Who was the first Christian martyr?
   Stephen

2. Define the word *witness* as used in the lesson.
   Attestation of a fact or event
   One who has a personal knowledge of something
   Someone called to give evidence in a court

3. Name four qualities of Stephen's character.
   Full of faith
   Full of power
   Irresistible wisdom
   Irresistible spirit

4. Is it possible to please God without faith?
   No, it is impossible to please God without faith. Hebrews 11:6 says, "But without faith it is impossible to please him...."

5. Where did the Jews who were unable to worship at the temple gather for worship and teaching?
   The Jews gathered in the Synagogues.

6. What word is often used in the Scriptures to describe our attitude or disposition?
   Spirit

7. In Daniel 6:3, why was Daniel preferred above all others?
   Because he had an excellent spirit.

LESSON SEVEN—A WITNESS MAKES A DIFFERENCE

8. Name some obstacles that hinder our being witnesses for Christ.
    Answers will vary. Unconfessed sin, confidence in our flesh instead of God, hesitation, busyness, etc.

9. Stephen's life particularly impacted what person mentioned in Acts 7 and 8?
    Saul

10. To whose declaration in death was Stephen's similar?
    Stephen's declaration, "Lord Jesus, receive my spirit" was similar to our Lord Jesus Christ's declaration, "Father, into thy hands I commend my spirit."

Memory Verse

HEBREWS 6:10
10 For God is not unrighteous to forget your work and labour of love, which ye have shewed toward his name, in that ye have ministered to the saints, and do minister.

LESSON EIGHT

Encouragement Makes a Difference

Key Verses

Acts 11:19–26

Lesson Theme

To make a difference, we must determine, as Barnabas, to encourage others with our words, actions, and testimonies.

Lesson Overview

In past lessons, we have uncovered seven characteristics present in the lives of these first generation Christians. By examining their relationships, both with one another and with those outside the church, we have seen their dauntless service to Christ in the midst of a hostile culture.

One man in particular made a difference by encouraging his fellow believers. His name was Barnabas. Glimpses of his encouraging nature, in addition to his encouragement as a missionary companion to Paul the Apostle, are seen as early as chapter 4 and continue throughout the book.

MAKING A DIFFERENCE

Teaching Outline

 I. The Place of Encouragement: Antioch
  A. The scattering of the persecuted
  B. The salvation of the pagans

 II. The Person of Encouragement: Barnabas
  A. Barnabas was glad.
  B. Barnabas was good.
  C. Barnabas was godly.
   1. Filled with the Holy Spirit
   2. Full of faith
  D. Barnabas was giving.

 III. The Product of Encouragement
  A. He helped a missionary get his start.
  B. He helped our movement get its name.

LESSON EIGHT

Encouragement Makes a Difference

Text

Acts 11:19–26

Introduction

Everyone has at least two names—the name given to him by his parents and the name given to him by those who have observed his life.

Barnabas was literally given a new name—which stuck—by those who observed his life. It was a "good name" (Proverbs 22:1). In Acts 4:36, the apostles said, in effect, "We're not going to call you *Joses*. We're going to call you *Barnabas*, which means 'the son of consolation.'"

ACTS 4:36

36 And Joses, who by the apostles was surnamed Barnabas, (which is, being interpreted, The son of consolation,) a Levite, and of the country of Cyprus,

To *console* is to comfort, encourage, or edify. Barnabas was a man who lifted others up; he knew how to lighten burdens. Another New Testament term for this concept is *exhortation*. Romans 12:8 lists exhortation as a spiritual gift bestowed on certain Christians. Apparently Barnabas had this gift.

Hebrews tells Christians to *"exhort one another daily"* (3:13) and to do so *"...so much the more, as ye see the day approaching"* (10:25).

To learn how to be an encourager, let's examine the life of Barnabas. We will look at Acts 11 and a few other passages which shine light on his encouraging manner, revealing **three reasons Barnabas became known as an encourager.**

I.   The Place of Encouragement: Antioch

ACTS 11:19–21

19 Now they which were scattered abroad upon the persecution that arose about Stephen travelled as far as Phenice, and Cyprus, and Antioch, preaching the word to none but unto the Jews only.
20 And some of them were men of Cyprus and Cyrene, which, when they were come to Antioch, spake unto the Grecians, preaching the Lord Jesus.
21 And the hand of the Lord was with them: and a great number believed, and turned unto the Lord.

Christians today relate Antioch to the great missionary center of Acts 13. But that is not the Antioch of Acts 11.

LESSON EIGHT—ENCOURAGEMENT MAKES A DIFFERENCE

Christianity had not yet arrived at this city of 200,000 people, situated 300 miles north of Jerusalem. It was a city steeped in idol worship and filled with ungodly practices.

But new believers would soon be born—believers in desperate need of encouragement. Notice how the Gospel, and later Barnabas, arrived in Antioch.

A. The scattering of the persecuted (v. 19)

In Acts 8, Saul quickly transitions from bystander at the martyrdom of Stephen to a vehement threat against the Jerusalem congregation.

ACTS 8:1

1 And Saul was consenting unto his death. And at that time there was a great persecution against the church which was at Jerusalem; and they were all scattered abroad throughout the regions of Judaea and Samaria, except the apostles.

During this "scattering abroad," the church refused to be silenced about their newfound faith. They continued preaching the Gospel and leading their fellow Jews to Christ.

ACTS 8:4

4 Therefore they that were scattered abroad went every where preaching the word.

B. The salvation of the pagans (vv. 20–21)

In verse 19, their evangelism remained directed to *"the Jew first"* (Romans 1:16). But in verse 20 we see a major shift. The scattered Jewish believers began sharing the Gospel with Gentiles, who responded by eagerly receiving Christ.

These soulwinners had no doubt heard of Peter's visit to Cornelius (Acts 10) and of the door of salvation having been opened to non-Jews. Notice the Jerusalem church leaders' response to Peter's testimony of the first Gentile conversions of Acts 10.

ACTS 11:18

18 When they heard these things, they held their peace, and glorified God, saying, Then hath God also to the Gentiles granted repentance unto life.

Commentary on Acts 11:20–21

There was instant revival! The message was like water to a thirsty man, like bread to the starving. The Gentiles, worn out and wearied with their pagan superstitions, heartsick over the deadness of their gods and the debaucheries of their priests, instantly recognized the truth. The name of the Lord Jesus wrought an instant response in their souls. The hand of the Lord was with His people in proclaiming the saving, sovereign Name to the Gentiles. Soon Jews would be a permanent minority in the church as ever increasing numbers of Gentiles turned gratefully to Christ.—*Exploring Acts*, by John Phillips, Loizeaux 1986

II. The Person of Encouragement: Barnabas

ACTS 11:22–24

22 Then tidings of these things came unto the ears of the church which was in Jerusalem: and they sent forth Barnabas, that he should go as far as Antioch.

LESSON EIGHT—ENCOURAGEMENT MAKES A DIFFERENCE

23 *Who, when he came, and had seen the grace of God, was glad, and exhorted them all, that with purpose of heart they would cleave unto the Lord.*
24 *For he was a good man, and full of the Holy Ghost and of faith: and much people was added unto the Lord.*

When news of the revival among the Gentiles in Antioch came to Jerusalem, the believers there sought a trusted leader to travel to Antioch and assess the situation. They needed a man with a sensible head and a sincere heart, and they looked no further than Barnabas. Every Christian should aspire to be this kind of person. Notice four characteristics seen in Barnabas' life which made him an encourager.

A. *Barnabas was glad (v. 23).*

When Barnabas arrived on the scene in Antioch, he did not greet the new movement among the Gentiles with skepticism, pessimism, jealousy, or doubt. He was *glad* for their conversion. How encouraging he must have been!

May God teach us to be glad for one another, and *"Rejoice with them that do rejoice"* (Romans 12:15). May He retrain our demeanor to default to joyful, not only when things are going well for us, but especially when things are going well for others. Paul explains that this response is the only real option for those who are joined in the body of Christ.

1 CORINTHIANS 12:26
26 *And whether one member suffer, all the members suffer with it; or one member be honoured, all the members rejoice with it.*

B. Barnabas was good (v. 24).

What a simple yet important label to be given: *"He was a good man"* (v. 24). Can your family, neighbors, coworkers, and fellow Christians say this of you?

GALATIANS 6:10

10 *As we have therefore opportunity, let us do good unto all men, especially unto them who are of the household of faith.*

JAMES 4:17

17 *Therefore to him that knoweth to do good, and doeth it not, to him it is sin.*

Doing good is the one way all of us can follow Christ's example. Acts 10:38 says that our Saviour *"went about doing good."* Hebrews 13:16 tells us *"forget not"* to *"do good."* Third John 11 explains that doing good is one characteristic of those who are *"of God."*

C. Barnabas was godly (v. 24).

In addition to being a good man, Barnabas was also a godly man. The same terminology used to describe Stephen described him.

ACTS 6:5

5 *And the saying pleased the whole multitude: and they chose Stephen, a man full of faith and of the Holy Ghost, and Philip, and Prochorus, and Nicanor, and Timon, and Parmenas, and Nicolas a proselyte of Antioch:*

LESSON EIGHT—ENCOURAGEMENT MAKES A DIFFERENCE

1. Filled with the Spirit

A godly man depends on the Holy Spirit for the guidance and direction necessary to live a life consistent with the Word of God (see Ephesians 5:18).

2. Full of faith

A godly man is full of faith as a result of saturating his heart and mind with God's Word (see Romans 10:17).

D. Barnabas was giving.

In Acts 4, Barnabas sold a parcel of land that he had owned, likely on his home island of Cyprus. He took the proceeds of this sale and invested them into the work of the early church. His generosity enabled a young congregation to move forward in their growing work for God.

ACTS 4:36–37

36 And Joses, who by the apostles was surnamed Barnabas, (which is, being interpreted, The son of consolation,) a Levite, and of the country of Cyprus,

37 Having land, sold it, and brought the money, and laid it at the apostles' feet.

Barnabas actually believed the words of our Lord, *"It is more blessed to give than to receive"* (Acts 20:35). His eagerness to give was a means of great encouragement to the struggling believers in Jerusalem. Paul may have had Barnabas in mind when he wrote the following to the Corinthian church:

2 CORINTHIANS 9:7

7 Every man according as he purposeth in his heart, so let him give; not grudgingly, or of necessity: for God loveth a cheerful giver.

125

Paul gives four characteristics of those "rich in this world." Does Barnabas fit this description? 1) Not arrogant because of our resources. 2) Not trusting in wealth but in God. 3) Rich in good works. 4) Ready to distribute resources to others.

1 TIMOTHY 6:17–18
17 Charge them that are rich in this world, that they be not highminded, nor trust in uncertain riches, but in the living God, who giveth us richly all things to enjoy;
18 That they do good, that they be rich in good works, ready to distribute, willing to communicate;

III. The Product of Encouragement

ACTS 11:25–26
25 Then departed Barnabas to Tarsus, for to seek Saul:
26 And when he had found him, he brought him unto Antioch. And it came to pass, that a whole year they assembled themselves with the church, and taught much people. And the disciples were called Christians first in Antioch.

It's hard to measure what a little encouragement can do. We tend to underestimate the value of simple, thoughtful acts of encouragement. You never know what positive consequences your words or deeds of encouragement may produce. Consider the results of Barnabas' encouragement:

A. He helped a missionary get his start (v. 25).
Barnabas left Antioch, went to Tarsus to get Saul (soon to be re-named *Paul*), and returned with him to teach the new believers.

126

LESSON EIGHT—ENCOURAGEMENT MAKES A DIFFERENCE

This was the second record of these men being together. We learn from their relationship that Barnabas' encouragement was a great factor in Paul's entrance into the Gospel ministry.

ACTS 9:26–27

26 And when Saul was come to Jerusalem, he assayed to join himself to the disciples: but they were all afraid of him, and believed not that he was a disciple.
27 But Barnabas took him, and brought him to the apostles, and declared unto them how he had seen the Lord in the way, and that he had spoken to him, and how he had preached boldly at Damascus in the name of Jesus.

When Paul, the violent persecutor of the church, was converted, those who knew his reputation were hesitant to receive him into their fellowship. Some naturally concluded that he was a spy or pretender.

Barnabas, however, not only received Paul and believed his testimony but also personally introduced him to Peter, James, John, and others. Apparently Barnabas was well respected by the apostles, and when he brought Paul to them, there was a miraculous union between these weathered leaders and a fresh face of faith.

Romans 15:7 tells us, *"receive ye one another."* May the Lord enable us to take newcomers under our wings, show them the ropes, and help them as they start walking with Him. God is looking for encouraging Christians with whom He can entrust spiritual newborns. Will we receive and nurture them as Barnabas did with Paul?

You may not be the next "Apostle Paul," so to speak, but don't forget that you could be the encourager of the one who is. Maybe the next "Apostle Paul" is a child you teach in Sunday school or a first-time guest you will greet today or someone you will disciple. Maybe the next "Apostle Paul" is one of the children under your own roof!

B. He helped our movement get its name (v. 26).

Because Barnabas labored, mentored, and invested in the lives of the Christians in Antioch, they were grounded in their faith and nurtured into committed disciples. In fact, their church became a thriving center for missions and influenced much of the apostles' work throughout the remainder of the book of Acts.

In Antioch the believers were given a new name, not chosen by them but by their enemies. The citizens of Antioch, as they observed the lives of the believers, called them *Christians* for the first time, coining a term that endures two millennia later. *Christian*, of course, means "Christ-like ones" or "Christ followers." It fits since God's express will for His children is to be conformed into the image of His Son (Romans 8:29).

Leading people to become like Christ is not an easy task, but Paul and Barnabas worked with these folks to that end. This became the pattern of Paul's ministry—laboring in the lives of people until it could be said of them that they had become like Christ.

GALATIANS 4:19

19 My little children, of whom I travail in birth again until Christ be formed in you,

LESSON EIGHT—ENCOURAGEMENT MAKES A DIFFERENCE

Conclusion

Are you an encourager to those around you?

Hymn

George Shuler and Ira Wilson were roommates at Moody Bible Institute in 1924. At the institute, they combined their talents and gave the world a beautiful song of consecration, "Make Me A Blessing." Wilson wrote the lyrics, Shuler the music.

At first the song was rejected by music publishers, so Shuler had one thousand copies printed to distribute on his own. One fell into the hands of George Dibble, an outstanding singer who was, at that time, music director for the International Sunday School Convention in Cleveland, Ohio. Dibble asked for permission to use the song, and it was granted. Soon people everywhere were singing the song, and publishers wanted to distribute copies.

Between the time Ira Wilson wrote the lyrics and the time the song became well known, Wilson apparently forgot that he was the author! Until he died, he never remembered that he had written these famous words.

Make Me a Blessing
Out in the highways and byways of life,
Many are weary and sad;
Carry the sunshine where darkness is rife,
Making the sorrowing glad.

Make me a blessing, Make me a blessing,
Out of my life, May Jesus shine;
Make me a blessing, O Savior, I pray,
Make me a blessing to someone today.

Tell the sweet story of Christ and His love;
Tell of His power to forgive;
Others will trust Him if only you prove
True every moment you live.

Give as 'twas given to you in your need;
Love as the Master loved you,
Be to the helpless a helper indeed;
Unto your mission be true.

May we live each day with this prayer on our hearts, *"Lord, make me a blessing to someone today."*

LESSON EIGHT—ENCOURAGEMENT MAKES A DIFFERENCE

Study Questions

1. To what city was Barnabas sent to encourage the new Christians?
    Antioch

2. According to Acts 8:4, what did the Christians do when they were scattered?
    They preached the Word.

3. What are four characteristics that made Barnabas an encouragement?
    He was glad.

    He was good.

    He was godly.

    He was giving.

4. In verse 24 of our text, Barnabas was labeled a "good man." What kind of label would others give you? Would your children, neighbors, coworkers, and fellow Christians be able to say the same about you?
    Answers will vary

5. From our lesson, what are the two characteristics that describe Barnabas as a godly man?
    He was filled with the Spirit.

    He was full of faith.

6. In Acts 4, what did Barnabas sell to invest in the work of the church?
    A piece of land

MAKING A DIFFERENCE

7. A little encouragement can go a long way. What are some small, practical ways you can be an encouragement to someone today?
    Answers will vary.

8. Whom did Barnabas help to get started in Christian ministry?
    The Apostle Paul

9. In the past week, how have you been an encouragement to those around you?
    Answers will vary.

10. In the past week, how has someone been an encouragement to you, personally?
    Answers will vary.

Memory Verse

GALATIANS 6:10
10 As we have therefore opportunity, let us do good unto all men, especially unto them who are of the household of faith.

LESSON NINE

Giving Makes a Difference

Key Verses

Acts 11:27–30

Lesson Theme

To make a difference, we must cultivate the grace of giving to meet the needs of others and the needs of God's work.

Lesson Overview

Generosity is a characteristic that we see demonstrated by the first generation Christians. In Acts 2, those converted on the day of Pentecost *"sold their possessions and goods, and parted them to all men, as every man had need"* (v. 45). Then in Acts 4, Barnabas *"Having land, sold it, and brought the money, and laid it at the apostles' feet"* (v. 37).

This time in Acts 11, we see the Christians in Antioch displaying generosity. When they discovered others' needs, they naturally responded with the same generosity that they had learned from their brothers and sisters in Christ—the generosity characteristic of genuine Christianity.

Teaching Outline

I. The Presence of a Need
   A. An accurate prophecy
   B. An acute poverty

II. The Participation in the Offering
   A. The people who gave—"every man"
   B. The proportion they gave—"according to his ability"
   C. The purpose they gave—"relief unto the brethren"

III. The Pattern for New Testament Giving
   A. Systematic giving
   B. Sacrificial giving
   C. Sincere giving
      1. Sincerity means a willing heart.
      2. Sincerity means a loving heart.
      3. Sincerity means a joyful heart.

LESSON NINE

Giving Makes a Difference

Text

Acts 11:27–30

Introduction

We're learning from the first-century Christians how to make a difference. We learned about *caring* from Peter and James, *witnessing* from Stephen, and *encouraging* from Barnabas.

In this lesson we will learn from the Christians in Antioch, the first major group of Gentiles who turned to Christ. As Acts 11 closes, these new believers are faced with an opportunity—to meet a need, to participate in an offering—an opportunity to give.

Illustration

One researcher asked children for their "instructions on life." They replied as follows:

- "Never trust a dog to watch your food."—Patrick, age 10
- "When you want something expensive, ask your grandparents."—Matthew, age 12
- "Wear a hat when feeding seagulls."—Rocky, age 9
- "Never try to hide a piece of broccoli in a glass of milk."—Rosemary, age 7
- "Never ask for anything that costs more than five dollars when your parents are doing taxes."—Carroll, age 9
- "Don't pick on your sister when she's holding a baseball bat."—Joel, age 12
- "Never try to baptize a cat."—Laura, age 13
- "When your dad is mad and asks you, 'Do I look stupid?' don't answer him."—Heather, age 16
- "Never tell your mom her diet is not working." —Michael, age 14

Today we will learn an instruction on life from the first-century Christians—giving makes a difference. Generosity is one of the great hallmark characteristics of God's people, and we will see it actively present in the offering given by the Antioch Christians.

We discover *three lessons from this extraordinary act of generosity.*

LESSON NINE—GIVING MAKES A DIFFERENCE

I. The Presence of a Need

ACTS 11:28

28 *And there stood up one of them named Agabus, and signified by the Spirit that there should be great dearth throughout all the world: which came to pass in the days of Claudius Caesar.*

This great famine was prophesied to cover the entire Roman Empire and beyond. Of course, this would affect the first-century Christians, all of whom, at this point, lived within the borders of this region.

A. An accurate prophecy

The first Christians to arrive in Antioch were those who had been scattered by persecution. Then Barnabas came, and after exhorting them, he and Paul spent a year discipling them. Now, we read that prophets have come to Antioch.

Commentary on New Testament Prophets

The New Testament gift of prophecy was unique to the early church. It was expressed by direct inspiration of the Spirit of God. It was a transitional gift of great value until the New Testament had been written and put into circulation, after which it ceased to be relevant. For the most part, like their Old Testament counterparts, New Testament prophets were "forth tellers" rather than foretellers. Their function was to communicate to local congregations truth revealed by the Spirit and relevant to present needs.—*Exploring Acts,* by John Phillips, Loizeaux 1986

One of these prophets, Agabus, spoke a prophecy that arrested the people's attention. He predicted a famine

137

that would spread throughout the entire known world. Many would suffer and die. Luke added that this prophecy later came true under the reign of Claudius Caesar.

B. An acute poverty

Poverty is no stranger to Christian people. Jesus divulged that He had no place to lay His head (Matthew 8:20). A study of world history bears out that people in every generation all over the world have experienced seasons of scarcity. And in each generation, Christians have endured these hardships. Paul testified that he knew what it meant to go hungry.

PHILIPPIANS 4:11–12

11 Not that I speak in respect of want: for I have learned, in whatsoever state I am, therewith to be content.
12 I know both how to be abased, and I know how to abound: every where and in all things I am instructed both to be full and to be hungry, both to abound and to suffer need.

Some, in the midst of financial difficulty, conclude that God has forgotten or forsaken them. This view of life is unrealistic. While some Christians have suffered poverty, others have suffered much more grave circumstances:

HEBREWS 11:36–38

36 And others had trial of cruel mockings and scourgings, yea, moreover of bonds and imprisonment:
37 They were stoned, they were sawn asunder, were tempted, were slain with the sword: they wandered about in sheepskins and goatskins; being destitute, afflicted, tormented;
38 (Of whom the world was not worthy:) they wandered in deserts, and in mountains, and in dens and caves of the earth.

LESSON NINE—GIVING MAKES A DIFFERENCE

If you are wondering how God is going to meet the pressing needs in your life, remember that you are in good company. Job, Joseph, and a host of others had needs and waited patiently for God's provision. At times, God provides no explanation for our suffering. We must trust that our Father knows best, that He will see us through, and that He will work the entire situation for our good (Romans 8:28).

II. The Participation in the Offering

ACTS 11:29

29 Then the disciples, every man according to his ability, determined to send relief unto the brethren which dwelt in Judaea:

The Antioch Christians, though they were relatively new in their faith, determined to help those affected by this famine. They saw the need and took the lead!

A. The people who gave—"every man"

How wonderful is the spirit in ministry when *everyone* does *something.* Rarely would two people give the same size gift. But when everyone in the group has the same size heart, we're getting somewhere.

Giving was never meant for a select few within the body of Christ. It is a team effort, and everyone can play a role. Since giving is part of our spiritual growth, and we all want to grow, then we must all determine to give.

1 CORINTHIANS 16:2A

*2A Upon the first day of the week let **every one of you** lay by him in store, as God hath prospered him,*

Moses encouraged the same level of participation:

DEUTERONOMY 16:17

17 **Every man** shall give as he is able, according to the blessing of the LORD thy God which he hath given thee.

Illustration

Being a part of the original group that helped to launch Apple computer, Ronald Wayne sold his ten percent interest in the company for $800. Getting cold feet and lacking a vision for Apple's future, he failed to take the initial investment risk and focus on the long-term dividend. That $800 investment would be worth more than $300 million today. —*Houston Chronicle*, July 23, 1999, sec. 5F

B. The proportion they gave—"according to his ability"

The offering in Antioch had a common characteristic with other Bible offerings: the participation was to vary by individual, based on the unique enabling of God in the life of each person.

No one is in competition with anyone else, and no one should compare himself with anyone else (2 Corinthians 10:12). Individuals are responsible and accountable for doing what God would have them to do with what He has entrusted to them.

Jesus commended the widow, not because her amount was larger, but because her sacrifice was greater.

Lesson Nine—Giving Makes a Difference

Mark 12:41–44

41 And Jesus sat over against the treasury, and beheld how the people cast money into the treasury: and many that were rich cast in much.

42 And there came a certain poor widow, and she threw in two mites, which make a farthing.

43 And he called unto him his disciples, and saith unto them, Verily I say unto you, That this poor widow hath cast more in, than all they which have cast into the treasury:

44 For all they did cast in of their abundance; but she of her want did cast in all that she had, even all her living.

See again the instruction of Moses.

Deuteronomy 16:17

*17 Every man shall give **as he is able, according to the blessing of the LORD** thy God which he hath given thee.*

Later, when Paul gave instructions regarding another offering for Jerusalem, he made it clear that giving is not a one-size-fits-all proposition.

2 Corinthians 8:12–15

12 For if there be first a willing mind, it is accepted according to that a man hath, and not according to that he hath not.

13 For I mean not that other men be eased, and ye burdened:

14 But by an equality, that now at this time your abundance may be a supply for their want, that their abundance also may be a supply for your want: that there may be equality:

15 As it is written, He that had gathered much had nothing over; and he that had gathered little had no lack.

Great news—no one is expected to give something he doesn't have (v. 12)! This issue of proportionate giving should encourage every Christian who finds himself in difficult circumstances. There's no place for guilt or competition in this environment.

Illustration

Some people resort to earthly and carnal methods both in gaining money and in giving money. Some folks have every intention to give...just as soon as they win the lottery! God doesn't want me to give some large gift someday when *chance* makes me able. He wants me to give a proportionate gift today from the resources He has provided.

Someone once defined the words *state lottery* in this way: "A tax on people who are bad at math."

Someone else asked the question, "Have you ever noticed how people who spend all their money on beer, cigarettes, and lottery tickets seem to constantly complain about being broke and not feeling well?"

C. The purpose they gave—"relief unto the brethren"

The children's song says it well: "Sharing, sharing, that's what Christians do!"

Generosity does not come naturally. We must fight against the worldly tendencies of protecting self and "looking out for number one."

The Antioch Christians could have reasoned, "Well, Agabus said the famine would come to the whole world. That includes us in Antioch. I had better save up for *my* rainy day." Instead they thought like this: "Others need it; I have it; I will share it."

God gives *to us* what He intends to flow *through* us.

They gave to help others. When we give through the ministry of the local church, we are helping others in a very real way. The local church meets peoples' needs—yes, their physical needs, but especially their spiritual needs. The church meets needs by giving food to those who need a meal, a lift to those who need a ride, a hand to those who need help, a visit to those who need a companion, and the Gospel to those who need salvation.

"Do good with what thou hast; or it will do thee no good."

—William Penn

Zacchaeus is a great case study for the difference that Jesus Christ makes in the area of one's giving. For his entire adult life as a Roman tax collector, Zacchaeus had "lived to get." But when he got saved, the first thing to change was his willingness to share his resources with others.

LUKE 19:8

8 *And Zacchaeus stood, and said unto the Lord; Behold, Lord, the half of my goods I give to the poor; and if I have taken any thing from any man by false accusation, I restore him fourfold.*

III. The Pattern for New Testament Giving

ACTS 11:30

30 *Which also they did, and sent it to the elders by the hands of Barnabas and Saul.*

This offering was neither the first nor the last offering of this nature. Offerings to meet the needs in the young and growing congregations began in Acts 2–4, and we continue to read about benevolent offerings in Philippians, 1 and 2 Corinthians, and throughout the life of the early church.

Throughout Paul's service as the great New Testament missionary, he received and distributed offerings as needed to struggling congregations.

These *three characteristics* would become part of the "Giving DNA" of the first-century churches.

A. Systematic giving

In the culture of the early church, giving soon became a matter of regularity. It did not have the same rigidity or compulsion as the Old Testament law. On the other hand, New Testament giving in no way took on a "Give what you can, when you can, if you can, when you feel like it," mentality.

1 CORINTHIANS 16:2
2 Upon the first day of the week let every one of you lay by him in store, as God hath prospered him, that there be no gatherings when I come.

A sure sign of Christian growth is faithfulness in giving. Maturing Christians work to become systematic—predictable and dependable—in their giving.

Illustration

Godfrey Davis, who wrote a biography about the Duke of Wellington, said, "I found an old account ledger that showed how the Duke spent his money. It was a far better clue to what he thought was really important than the

reading of his letters or speeches."—*Our Daily Bread,*
August 26, 1993

B. Sacrificial giving

In the early church, giving always included some measure
of sacrifice.

Paul used the Macedonians'
giving as an example to others.
Their giving did not come from an
overflow of abundance, but from
the depths of poverty.

> Some Christians
> give to God's work
> *weekly,* others
> just *weakly.*

2 CORINTHIANS 8:2
2   *How that in a great trial of affliction the abundance of
their joy and their deep poverty abounded unto the riches
of their liberality.*

Our Lord Jesus Christ serves as the ultimate example
when it comes to sacrifice:

2 CORINTHIANS 8:9
9   *For ye know the grace of our Lord Jesus Christ, that,
though he was rich, yet for your sakes he became poor, that
ye through his poverty might be rich.*

King David demonstrated this characteristic of
giving when he said to Araunah, *"Nay; but I will surely
buy it of thee at a price: neither will I offer burnt offerings
unto the LORD my God of that which doth cost me nothing"*
(2 Samuel 24:24).

C. Sincere giving

If giving is anything, it must be sincere. Motives do matter.
God does not need our gifts, but He wants a meaningful
act of worship from a sincere heart.

1. Sincerity means a willing heart.

God never intended His work to be supported by anything but a willing heart.

2 Corinthians 8:3, 12

3 For to their power, I bear record, yea, and beyond their power they were willing of themselves;

12 For if there be first a willing mind, it is accepted according to that a man hath, and not according to that he hath not.

When it came time to build the tabernacle, God presented, through Moses, a list of the materials required, including precious metals, dyed skins, exquisite fabrics, and valuable stones (Exodus 25:1–8). But the offering had one stipulation: willing hearts on the part of the givers.

Exodus 25:2

2 Speak unto the children of Israel, that they bring me an offering: of every man that giveth it willingly with his heart ye shall take my offering.

How did the Hebrews respond?

Exodus 35:21

21 And they came, every one whose heart stirred him up, and every one whom his spirit made willing, and they brought the Lord's offering to the work of the tabernacle of the congregation, and for all his service, and for the holy garments.

2. Sincerity means a loving heart.

You may say you love the Lord, but giving "puts your money where your mouth is." Love does many things

LESSON NINE—GIVING MAKES A DIFFERENCE

for the object of its affections—love serves, love pursues, love endures, and certainly, love gives.

2 CORINTHIANS 8:8

8 I speak not by commandment, but by occasion of the forwardness of others, and to prove the sincerity of your love.

The Lord Jesus may have the same question for us that He asked of Peter on the shores of Galilee following His resurrection, *"Simon, son of Jonas, lovest thou me more than these?"* (John 21:15).

3. Sincerity means a joyful heart.

When you truly love someone, you *enjoy* giving to him or her. We find great joy in giving when we know that we have honored, obeyed, and pleased our Lord, the one who has given so much for us.

2 CORINTHIANS 9:7

7 Every man according as he purposeth in his heart, so let him give; not grudgingly, or of necessity: for God loveth a cheerful giver.

Again, David demonstrates the heart of a sincere giver. After Israel had given their gigantic offering for the preparation of the temple, King David responded in humble joy.

1 CHRONICLES 29:13–14

13 Now therefore, our God, we thank thee, and praise thy glorious name.

> *"You can give without loving, but you cannot love without giving."*
> —Amy Carmichael

147

14 But who am I, and what is my people, that we should be able to offer so willingly after this sort? for all things come of thee, and of thine own have we given thee.

Conclusion

Money is simply a tool that God has provided to get His work done on Earth. It's also a test of our relationship with Him. How we handle money demonstrates how much we trust Him. We must acknowledge His ownership of it all and seek to follow His leadership in managing each dollar He entrusts to us. If we follow His lead, we can make a difference—through giving.

Quote

The Limits of Money
Money will buy...
A bed but not sleep;
Books but not brains;
Food but not appetite;
Finery but not beauty;
A house but not a home;
Medicine but not health;
Luxuries but not culture;
Amusements but not happiness;
Religion but not salvation;
A passport to many places but not Heaven.
—The Voice in the Wilderness, quoted in *Discipleship Journal*, Issue 53, 1989, pg. 21

LESSON NINE—GIVING MAKES A DIFFERENCE

Study Questions

1. Which prophet spoke of a famine that would spread throughout the entire known world?
    Agabus

2. According to verse 29, how many people gave?
    Every man

3. Does God require every person to give the same amount? Use Scripture to support your answer.
    God does not require every person to give the same amount. While God requires all Christians to give, He is concerned with our heart attitude, rather than the size of our gift. The widow in Mark 12:42 gave all she had—two mites, yet she gave more than the rich men because her sacrifice was greater. Also Deuteronomy 16:17.

4. For what purpose did the Christians give?
    For relief unto the brethren; for meeting needs

5. What pattern for New Testament giving was set in Antioch?
    Systematic giving
    Sacrificial giving
    Sincere giving

6. According to 1 Corinthians 16:2, on what day of each week are we instructed to give?
    Sunday, the first day of the week

149

7. What are the three characteristics of sincere giving?
   A willing heart

   A loving heart

   A joyful heart

8. It is possible to give without loving, but it is impossible to love without doing what?
   Giving

9. Where does giving to the Lord's work rank in your personal priorities?
   Answers will vary.

Memory Verse

2 CORINTHIANS 9:7
7 Every man according as he purposeth in his heart, so let him give; not grudgingly, or of necessity: for God loveth a cheerful giver.

LESSON TEN

Prayer Makes a Difference

Key Verse

Acts 12:1–19

Lesson Theme

To make a difference, we must be a people of consistent, faith-filled prayer.

Lesson Overview

We have learned from the first generation of Christians the difference they made by caring, witnessing, and giving. Today we will focus on praying—the foundational discipline of all that God accomplished through the life and ministry of the early church. If our churches today will make a difference, then prayer must be our foundation as well.

Teaching Outline

I. The Reason for their Prayers
   A. The growth of Herod's persecution
   B. The grief over James' martyrdom
   C. The gravity of Peter's imprisonment

II. God's Response to their Prayers
   A. He responded at the right time.
   B. He responded in the right place.
   C. He responded in the right way.

III. The Results of their Prayers
   A. The enemy's plans were thwarted.
   B. The church's prayers were interrupted.
   C. The ruler's guards were executed.

LESSON TEN

Prayer Makes a Difference

Text

Acts 12:1–19

Introduction

Prayer is non-negotiable if we seek to please God.

HEBREWS 11:6

6   But without faith it is impossible to please him: for he that cometh to God must believe that he is, and that he is a rewarder of them that diligently seek him.

Are you diligently seeking Him? Do you pray faithfully for the needs in your life and in the lives of others? Can God look forward to hearing your voice in prayer tomorrow morning?

PSALM 5:3

3   My voice shalt thou hear in the morning, O LORD; in the morning will I direct my prayer unto thee, and will look up.

Acts chapter 12 was a critical season in the life of the early church. And from their behavior, we glean *three perspectives on the prayers of God's people.*

I.   The Reason for their Prayers

ACTS 12:1–5

1   Now about that time Herod the king stretched forth his hands to vex certain of the church.

2   And he killed James the brother of John with the sword.

3   And because he saw it pleased the Jews, he proceeded further to take Peter also. (Then were the days of unleavened bread.)

4   And when he had apprehended him, he put him in prison, and delivered him to four quaternions of soldiers to keep him; intending after Easter to bring him forth to the people.

5   Peter therefore was kept in prison: but prayer was made without ceasing of the church unto God for him.

"The place and power of prayer in the Christian life is too little understood. When we learn to regard it as the highest part of the work entrusted to us—the root and strength of all other work—we will see that there is nothing we need to study and practice more than the art of praying."

—Andrew Murray

Prayer ought to come as naturally to the Christian as breathing, for it is just as necessary. But in some cases today, God must use trials to drive a believer to the place of prayer. If you are going through difficulty, don't be discouraged. God

LESSON TEN—PRAYER MAKES A DIFFERENCE

is waiting with open arms to comfort and help His children who reach out to Him in distress.

PSALM 50:15
15 And call upon me in the day of trouble: I will deliver thee, and thou shalt glorify me.

PSALM 86:7
7 In the day of my trouble I will call upon thee: for thou wilt answer me.

Learning to pray during a crisis is good, but it is even better to stay in the place of prayer after the crisis, maintaining a walk with God.

> Philippians 4:6 teaches us to worry about *nothing,* be thankful for *anything,* and pray about *everything.*

A. The growth of Herod's persecution (v. 1)

Herod Agrippa I was the grandson of Herod the Great. He was an insecure ruler appointed by Rome and, like most of his family, unpopular with the Jewish people. He saw the early Christians as an easy and expendable target he could use to win popularity with his subjects.

In such a difficult hour, prayer became the great resource to which God's people turned. When we experience fear, when we are tempted to retaliate or manipulate, when the situation is beyond our control, God's solution is always prayer.

PHILIPPIANS 4:6
6 Be careful for nothing; but in every thing by prayer and supplication with thanksgiving let your requests be made known unto God.

Are you looking for help in your time of need? God invites you to come to Him.

HEBREWS 4:16

16 Let us therefore come boldly unto the throne of grace, that we may obtain mercy, and find grace to help in time of need.

B. The grief over James' martyrdom (v. 2)

James, the son of Zebedee, was the first apostle to be martyred.

You may remember the occasion when James' mother requested special treatment for her two sons. Jesus asked the men, *"Are ye able to drink of the cup that I shall drink of, and to be baptized with the baptism that I am baptized with?"* (Matthew 20:22). They answered Him, *"We are able."* Now James had been given the opportunity to demonstrate his sincerity.

No doubt, the Christians' hearts were broken over the tragic loss of James. In times of grief, loss, or confusion, we must remember to go to the Lord in prayer. As a Father, He cares for us and seeks to welcome us into His comforting and loving arms.

1 PETER 5:7

7 Casting all your care upon him; for he careth for you.

PSALM 61:2

2 From the end of the earth will I cry unto thee, when my heart is overwhelmed: lead me to the rock that is higher than I.

C. The gravity of Peter's imprisonment (vv. 3–4)

Herod knew that Peter's death would please the Jews, just as James' death had. After all, they had commanded Peter to cease preaching the name of Jesus, but with no success.

LESSON TEN—PRAYER MAKES A DIFFERENCE

This was a grave situation. Paul referred to Peter as one of the "pillars" of the church in Jerusalem (Galatians 2:9). He had preached on Pentecost and had become a great pastoral leader in the church. How would they go on if they lost two of their leaders in such a short period of time?

The gravity of the situation impelled the Christians to pray *"without ceasing"* (v. 5). We must learn from the example of the early church about importunity in prayer. *Importunity* simply means "persistence." Jesus illustrated this for His disciples:

LUKE 11:5–9

5   *And he said unto them, Which of you shall have a friend, and shall go unto him at midnight, and say unto him, Friend, lend me three loaves;*

6   *For a friend of mine in his journey is come to me, and I have nothing to set before him?*

7   *And he from within shall answer and say, Trouble me not: the door is now shut, and my children are with me in bed; I cannot rise and give thee.*

8   *I say unto you, Though he will not rise and give him, because he is his friend, yet because of his importunity he will rise and give him as many as he needeth.*

9   *And I say unto you, Ask, and it shall be given you; seek, and ye shall find; knock, and it shall be opened unto you.*

Sometimes our prayers remain unanswered simply because we give up far too soon.

II. God's Response to their Prayers

God responds to the prayers of His people. Notice the great turn of events that began in the conclusion of verse 5: *"but prayer was made without ceasing of the church unto God for him.*" Consider the lessons learned from this single verse:

"but prayer was made"—a pivotal conjunction
"without ceasing"—a persevering commitment
"of the church"—a pleading company
"unto God"—a powerful Creator
"for him"—a personal concern

The *people's intercession* prompted *God's intervention*.

ACTS 12:6–10

6   And when Herod would have brought him forth, the same night Peter was sleeping between two soldiers, bound with two chains: and the keepers before the door kept the prison.

7   And, behold, the angel of the Lord came upon him, and a light shined in the prison: and he smote Peter on the side, and raised him up, saying, Arise up quickly. And his chains fell off from his hands.

8   And the angel said unto him, Gird thyself, and bind on thy sandals. And so he did. And he saith unto him, Cast thy garment about thee, and follow me.

9   And he went out, and followed him; and wist not that it was true which was done by the angel; but thought he saw a vision.

10 When they were past the first and the second ward, they came unto the iron gate that leadeth unto the city; which opened to them of his own accord: and they went out, and passed on through one street; and forthwith the angel departed from him.

A. He responded at the right time.

God's intervention occurred *"when Herod would have brought him forth."* It has been estimated that Peter spent

LESSON TEN—PRAYER MAKES A DIFFERENCE

approximately a week in prison. Peter was used to being on the move, but this week required him to exercise patience. And on the very night before Herod planned to take Peter's life, God sent His angel.

Many people whom God used greatly were required to trust God's timing in their lives. **Abraham** was required to wait for the promised son. **Joseph** waited while in prison. **David** waited after having been anointed king. **Job** waited while enduring pain and loss.

JOB 23:10
10 *But he knoweth the way that I take: when he hath tried me, I shall come forth as gold.*

While waiting, remember that God is in control. He is wisely and carefully working all things to accomplish our good and His purposes.

GALATIANS 4:4
4 *But when the fulness of the time was come, God sent forth his Son, made of a woman, made under the law,*

ECCLESIASTES 3:1
1 *To every thing there is a season, and a time to every purpose under the heaven:*

B. He responded in the right place.
The angel of the Lord had no problem finding Peter in this cold, dark prison. Have you ever wondered if God knows where you are? He does! He knows right where you are, and exactly what you're experiencing.

1 PETER 3:12
12 *For the eyes of the Lord are over the righteous, and his ears are open unto their prayers: but the face of the Lord is against them that do evil.*

God did not forget His children during their season of difficulty in Egypt. He did not forget the Apostle Peter. And He will not forget you.

Exodus 3:7

7 And the Lord said, I have surely seen the affliction of my people which are in Egypt, and have heard their cry by reason of their taskmasters; for I know their sorrows;

C. He responded in the right way.

When Jesus taught His disciples to pray, He assured them *"your Father knoweth what things ye have need of, before ye ask him"* (Matthew 6:8).

We're familiar with the promise of Romans 8:28, but see the larger picture, as it relates to prayer, in verses 26–28. God knows exactly how to answer our prayers according to His divine power and wisdom, even when we don't know exactly what to ask.

Romans 8:26–28

26 Likewise the Spirit also helpeth our infirmities: for we know not what we should pray for as we ought: but the Spirit itself maketh intercession for us with groanings which cannot be uttered.

27 And he that searcheth the hearts knoweth what is the mind of the Spirit, because he maketh intercession for the saints according to the will of God.

28 And we know that all things work together for good to them that love God, to them who are the called according to his purpose.

May we develop the faith in God that rests confidently, assured that He knows what He's doing.

LESSON TEN—PRAYER MAKES A DIFFERENCE

III. The Results of their Prayers

As God responds to His people's prayers, let's see how the rest of the story unfolds.

ACTS 12:11–19

11 *And when Peter was come to himself, he said, Now I know of a surety, that the Lord hath sent his angel, and hath delivered me out of the hand of Herod, and from all the expectation of the people of the Jews.*

12 *And when he had considered the thing, he came to the house of Mary the mother of John, whose surname was Mark; where many were gathered together praying.*

13 *And as Peter knocked at the door of the gate, a damsel came to hearken, named Rhoda.*

14 *And when she knew Peter's voice, she opened not the gate for gladness, but ran in, and told how Peter stood before the gate.*

15 *And they said unto her, Thou art mad. But she constantly affirmed that it was even so. Then said they, It is his angel.*

16 *But Peter continued knocking: and when they had opened the door, and saw him, they were astonished.*

17 *But he, beckoning unto them with the hand to hold their peace, declared unto them how the Lord had brought him out of the prison. And he said, Go shew these things unto James, and to the brethren. And he departed, and went into another place.*

18 *Now as soon as it was day, there was no small stir among the soldiers, what was become of Peter.*

19 *And when Herod had sought for him, and found him not, he examined the keepers, and commanded that they should be put to death. And he went down from Judaea to Caesarea, and there abode.*

A. The enemy's plans were thwarted (v. 11).

Peter was indeed delivered. It was no dream after all! According to verses 6–10, God delivered Peter from sixteen soldiers, two chains, keepers of the prison, an iron gate, and two wards. Our God is truly a miracle-working, prayer-answering God.

It has been said, "Man proposes, but God disposes." It doesn't matter what a cruel ruler, a nagging neighbor, a temperamental supervisor, or Satan himself determines to do. What does matter for the Christian is what God determines to allow. The psalmist put it in perspective:

PSALM 2:2–4

2 The kings of the earth set themselves, and the rulers take counsel together, against the LORD, and against his anointed, saying,

3 Let us break their bands asunder, and cast away their cords from us.

4 He that sitteth in the heavens shall laugh: the Lord shall have them in derision.

David praised the Lord for His ability to deliver him, in spite of his enemies' plans.

PSALM 18:48

48 He delivereth me from mine enemies: yea, thou liftest me up above those that rise up against me: thou hast delivered me from the violent man.

B. The church's prayers were interrupted (vv. 12–17).

It's hard to keep a straight face while reading the account of Peter's arrival at the prayer meeting, held at Mary's house, where they were pleading for his release. (Mary

LESSON TEN—PRAYER MAKES A DIFFERENCE

was the sister of Barnabas and the mother of John Mark—the same John Mark who later traveled with Paul and Barnabas and wrote the Gospel of Mark.)

Their prayers were literally answered *while they were on their knees*—they couldn't believe it. To them, it was simply too good to be true!

This account illustrates that God answers the prayer of faith even when that faith is small or weak. Remember the burdened father who said to Jesus, *"Lord, I believe; help thou mine unbelief"* (Mark 9:24). Jesus responded by answering that man's prayer on behalf of his son.

The Old Testament prophets said to expect these beyond-expectation answers from our God:

ISAIAH 65:24
24 And it shall come to pass, that before they call, I will answer; and while they are yet speaking, I will hear.

JEREMIAH 33:3
3 Call unto me, and I will answer thee, and shew thee great and mighty things, which thou knowest not.

Paul told us to expect the same.

EPHESIANS 3:20
20 Now unto him that is able to do exceeding abundantly above all that we ask or think, according to the power that worketh in us,

C. The ruler's guards were executed (vv. 18–19).

According to the Justinian code, if a prisoner escaped, the guards responsible would suffer the punishment originally intended for the prisoner. This is exactly what occurred in verses 18–19.

163

David praised the Lord for turning the tables on his enemies.

PSALM 138:7

7   *Though I walk in the midst of trouble, thou wilt revive me: thou shalt stretch forth thine hand against the wrath of mine enemies, and thy right hand shall save me.*

Conclusion

God wants to work in our lives and on our behalf today. He wants to bless and use our church. He wants to protect and provide for our families. He says to us, *"I will work"* (Isaiah 43:13).

The question lies not in God's willingness to answer, but in our willingness to pray.

JAMES 4:2B

2B   *…ye have not, because ye ask not.*

LESSON TEN—PRAYER MAKES A DIFFERENCE

Study Questions

1. How does God's Word teach us to respond to trouble?
   Prayer

2. In Acts 12, why were the Christians praying?
   Herod's persecution

   James' martyrdom

   Peter's imprisonment

3. According to Psalm 61:2, where should we go when we are overwhelmed?
   To the Rock, the Lord Jesus Christ

4. What is a memorable way to communicate the three-fold message of Philippians 4:6?
   Worry about nothing; be thankful for anything; pray about everything.

5. According to Hebrews 4:16, how are Christians supposed to come before God's throne?
   Boldly

6. Who was the first apostle to be martyred?
   James, the son of Zebedee

7. In one word, what does *importunity* mean?
   Persistence

8. Describe the characteristics of God's response to the believers' prayers in Acts 12.
   He responded at the right time.

165

He responded in the right place.

He responded in the right way.

9. When Peter was released from prison and went to Mary's house, what were the believers there doing?
    They were praying for Peter's release.

10. God is willing to answer if we are willing to pray. How is your prayer life? Is there a prayer request you desperately need God to answer?
    Answers will vary.

Memory Verse

HEBREWS 11:6

6 *But without faith it is impossible to please him: for he that cometh to God must believe that he is, and that he is a rewarder of them that diligently seek him.*

LESSON ELEVEN

Missions Makes a Difference

Key Verses

Acts 13:1–14:28

Lesson Theme

To make a difference, we must send, support, and partner with missionaries who will go into all the world with the Gospel message. We must also be active ourselves in taking the Gospel to every person.

Lesson Overview

The first generation of Christians made a difference in the lives of those around them by seeing people saved, baptized, and discipled in their faith. They met one another's needs and showed compassion to those outside the church.

However, most of this effectual activity was occurring in a relatively small geographic area. The diameter of their influence would need to grow larger!

In this lesson we learn from Paul's first missionary journey, as recorded in Acts 13–14, about the importance of making a difference through missions—that is, crossing boundaries and taking the Gospel of Christ to those not yet reached.

Teaching Outline

I. The Character the Missionaries Possessed
   A. Men who were faithful in the church
   B. Men who fasted and prayed
   C. Men who were filled with the Spirit

II. The Cities the Missionaries Reached
   A. Salamis (Acts 13:5)
   B. Paphos (Acts 13:6–13)
   C. Antioch (Acts 13:14–52)
   D. Iconium (Acts 14:1–5)
   E. Lystra (Acts 14:6–20)
   F. Derbe (Acts 14:20–21)

III. The Churches the Missionaries Established
   A. They taught the new believers in the churches.
   B. They trained the new pastors in the churches.
   C. They traveled back to the church that sent them.

LESSON ELEVEN

Missions Makes
a Difference

Text

Acts 13:1–14:28

Introduction

There are two important lessons to consider when studying
the missionary endeavors of the early church. First, the
journey we study in this lesson was consistent with our Lord's
specific instructions to the disciples. He left them with the
responsibility to take His good news to regions far beyond
their own. And now, in AD 46 or 47, the first missionaries,
Paul and Barnabas, do just that. Remember what Jesus said
to the eleven before His ascension.

Making a Difference

ACTS 1:8

8 But ye shall receive power, after that the Holy Ghost is come upon you: and ye shall be witnesses unto me both in Jerusalem, and in all Judaea, and in Samaria, and unto the uttermost part of the earth.

Second, all of us—not just those on foreign fields—are missionaries, in the broad sense of the term. If a *missionary* is defined as "one who crosses boundaries to take the Gospel to those not yet reached," then God intends every Christian to be a missionary.

2 CORINTHIANS 5:19–20

19 To wit, that God was in Christ, reconciling the world unto himself, not imputing their trespasses unto them; and hath committed unto us the word of reconciliation.
20 Now then we are ambassadors for Christ, as though God did beseech you by us: we pray you in Christ's stead, be ye reconciled to God.

Illustration

One church that understood this concept had a sign posted over the exit doors to remind the congregation upon their departure each Sunday, **"You Are Now Entering the Mission Field."**

Will we make a difference through missions in the twenty-first century? If so, we must not only increasingly send and support church-planting missionaries to all corners of the earth but also *be* missionaries ourselves, around our own corners and across our own streets.

Here in Acts 13–14, we learn from the first missionary journey of the Apostle Paul *a three-fold strategy for New Testament Missions.*

LESSON ELEVEN—MISSIONS MAKES A DIFFERENCE

I. The Character the Missionaries Possessed

ACTS 13:1–5

1 Now there were in the church that was at Antioch certain prophets and teachers; as Barnabas, and Simeon that was called Niger, and Lucius of Cyrene, and Manaen, which had been brought up with Herod the tetrarch, and Saul.

2 As they ministered to the Lord, and fasted, the Holy Ghost said, Separate me Barnabas and Saul for the work whereunto I have called them.

3 And when they had fasted and prayed, and laid their hands on them, they sent them away.

4 So they, being sent forth by the Holy Ghost, departed unto Seleucia; and from thence they sailed to Cyprus.

5 And when they were at Salamis, they preached the word of God in the synagogues of the Jews: and they had also John to their minister.

Reaching people for Christ begins with the character of those on the sending side of the equation. As we endeavor to reach others with the Gospel, we must determine to be a *"vessel unto honour, sanctified, and meet for the master's use"* (2 Timothy 2:21). This call to character is issued to every man and woman who desires to be used of God.

In the church at Antioch, two godly men were selected from the congregation to be missionaries—Paul and Barnabas. Notice three characteristics of these men.

A. Men who were faithful in the church (vv. 13:1–2)

Verse 1 says they were *"in the church"* and that they were already involved, teaching others. Then, verse 2 further

171

explains that they *"ministered to the Lord."* These were not self-appointed, ministry entrepreneurs. They were proven, faithful, steady men.

Years later, when Paul wrote Timothy, he recalled the importance of this characteristic.

1 Timothy 1:12

12 And I thank Christ Jesus our Lord, who hath enabled me, for that he counted me faithful, putting me into the ministry;

Every Christian man ought to strive to live before believers and non-believers alike in such a way that it could be said, "He is a faithful man!" The world has seen enough flash-in-the-pan, fizzled-out Christians. May we determine to be men of faithful service and steady devotion.

Proverbs 28:20

20 A faithful man shall abound with blessings: but he that maketh haste to be rich shall not be innocent.

B. Men who fasted and prayed (vv. 13:2–3)

Prayer is the great foundation for all Christian ministry. Without it we can bear no real fruit, see no lasting results, and accomplish nothing of eternal significance.

When the disciples found themselves unable to meet the need of a burdened father, Jesus explained to them the cause for their powerlessness.

Matthew 17:20–21

20 And Jesus said unto them, Because of your unbelief: for verily I say unto you, If ye have faith as a grain of mustard seed, ye shall say unto this mountain, Remove hence to yonder place; and it shall remove; and nothing shall be impossible unto you.

LESSON ELEVEN—MISSIONS MAKES A DIFFERENCE

21 *Howbeit this kind goeth not out but by prayer and fasting.*

C. Men who were filled with the Spirit (vv. 13:4–5)

The fullness of the Spirit was not intended just for Paul and Barnabas. Every Christian, in every age, is commanded to be filled with the Spirit.

> Before we talk to the people about God, we should talk to God about the people.

EPHESIANS 5:18

18 *And be not drunk with wine, wherein is excess; but be filled with the Spirit;*

How do you become filled with the Spirit? By abiding with Christ in prayer and in the Word, emptying yourself of sin, pride, and self, and asking Him to fill you, yielding yourself to His control (John 15:1–8).

How can someone tell if you're filled with the Spirit? By demonstrating the fruit only He can fully produce: love, joy, peace, longsuffering, gentleness, goodness, faith, meekness, and temperance (Galatians 5:22–23).

II. The Cities the Missionaries Reached

As Paul and Barnabas were sent on their way, they reached people with the Gospel in the following six cities:

A. Salamis (v. 13:5)

ACTS 13:5

5 *And when they were at Salamis, they preached the word of God in the synagogues of the Jews: and they had also John to their minister.*

173

Salamis was a city on the east coast of the island of Cyprus. This island, approximately 60 miles wide and 140 miles long, lies in the eastern portion of the Mediterranean Sea. It was here that Barnabas had previously sold land to help meet the needs of the young congregation in Jerusalem (Acts 4:36–37). Now he returned to his homeland as a missionary.

The focal point of New Testament missions is delivering the Word of God. Every local church and individual Christian must strive to accomplish this task. Whether you teach a Sunday school class, visit in a rest home, drive a church bus, or give to missions, your primary objective is to introduce the Word of God to those who need to hear it.

Paul also emphasized the central role of the Word of God.

1 THESSALONIANS 2:13

13 For this cause also thank we God without ceasing, because, when ye received the word of God which ye heard of us, ye received it not as the word of men, but as it is in truth, the word of God, which effectually worketh also in you that believe.

MISSIONS INSIGHT FROM SALAMIS

Their ministry in the city of Salamis teaches us about their **purpose***: "they preached the Word of God" (v. 5).*

B. Paphos (vv. 13:6–13)

ACTS 13:6–7

6 And when they had gone through the isle unto Paphos, they found a certain sorcerer, a false prophet, a Jew, whose name was Barjesus:

Lesson Eleven—Missions Makes a Difference

7   Which was with the deputy of the country, Sergius Paulus, a prudent man; who called for Barnabas and Saul, and desired to hear the word of God.

After traveling the length of the island, Paul's team arrived in Paphos on the west coast of Cyprus. Paphos was the capital city and the base of operations for the Roman government on the island.

After encountering a Roman deputy with an open heart, Paul, Barnabas, and their traveling companion John Mark were confronted by a wicked sorcerer who attempted to hinder their ministry. But because these men were filled and empowered by the Holy Spirit, not only was the sorcerer confounded and even blinded, but the deputy was saved (v. 12).

Whenever the work of God moves forward—whether in the life of one Christian or the ministry of an entire church—we can expect spiritual opposition. The devil hates his territory being conquered by the Lord Jesus Christ. He does not surrender ground easily.

Ephesians 6:11–12

11   Put on the whole armour of God, that ye may be able to stand against the wiles of the devil.

12   For we wrestle not against flesh and blood, but against principalities, against powers, against the rulers of the darkness of this world, against spiritual wickedness in high places.

MISSIONS INSIGHT FROM PAPHOS

*Their ministry in the city of Paphos teaches us of this team's recurring **problem** of spiritual opposition: "But Elymas the sorcerer...withstood them" (v. 8).*

MAKING A DIFFERENCE

C. Antioch (vv. 13:14–52)
ACTS 13:14
14 But when they departed from Perga, they came to Antioch in Pisidia, and went into the synagogue on the sabbath day, and sat down.

After the deputy's salvation in Paphos, the team sailed north in the Mediterranean to the seaport Perga, journeying to Antioch, a city in the region known as Pisidia (Asia Minor, or modern day Turkey). Many ancient cities were named Antioch. This city is different from the Antioch from which Paul and Barnabas were sent.

The heart of chapter 13 records Paul's great Gospel sermon delivered outside the synagogue. This sermon was so anointed that the next week *"came almost the whole city together to hear the word of God"* (v. 44). Of course, some of the Jews did not like the message of Jesus, the Messiah. So as Paul turned his attention to the Gentiles, the Bible tells us that *"they were glad, and glorified the word of the Lord: and as many as were ordained to eternal life believed"* (v. 48).

Preaching is God's choice method for reaching people with the Gospel.

1 CORINTHIANS 1:21
21 For after that in the wisdom of God the world by wisdom knew not God, it pleased God by the foolishness of preaching to save them that believe.

MISSIONS INSIGHT FROM ANTIOCH

*Their ministry in the city of Antioch teaches us about Paul's **preaching**: "Then Paul stood up, and beckoning with his hand said…" (v. 16).*

LESSON ELEVEN—MISSIONS MAKES A DIFFERENCE

D. Iconium (vv. 14:1–5)
ACTS 14:1–3

1   And it came to pass in Iconium, that they went both together into the synagogue of the Jews, and so spake, that a great multitude both of the Jews and also of the Greeks believed.
2   But the unbelieving Jews stirred up the Gentiles, and made their minds evil affected against the brethren.
3   Long time therefore abode they speaking boldly in the Lord, which gave testimony unto the word of his grace, and granted signs and wonders to be done by their hands.

Traveling southeast from Antioch—having been driven away by a growing and angry mob of Jews—Paul and Barnabas arrived in the city of Iconium. According to the *Holman Bible Dictionary*, today this city is known as Konya, the provincial capital of Turkey.

The response in Iconium was similar to other cities where Paul and Barnabas took the Gospel. At first, a great number believed (v. 1). But shortly after, troubled and entrenched religious leaders stirred up the people, causing great danger (v. 2). In spite of this, for a *"long time"* (v. 3) the men preached *"boldly"* in this city. It was not until the people literally picked up stones to cast at the missionary team that they moved on to Lystra (vv. 5–6).

Paul and Barnabas were righteous men, with the right message. They would not be intimidated.

MISSIONS INSIGHT FROM ICONIUM

Their ministry in the city of Iconium teaches us of the spiritual **power** *these soulwinners possessed: "speaking boldly in the Lord" (v. 3).*

177

MAKING A DIFFERENCE

PROVERBS 28:1

1   The wicked flee when no man pursueth: but the righteous are bold as a lion.

E. Lystra (vv. 14:6–20)

ACTS 14:8–10

8   And there sat a certain man at Lystra, impotent in his feet, being a cripple from his mother's womb, who never had walked:

9   The same heard Paul speak: who stedfastly beholding him, and perceiving that he had faith to be healed,

10   Said with a loud voice, Stand upright on thy feet. And he leaped and walked.

Traveling further south, the men arrived in Lystra. After a miraculous start with the healing of a lame man, the ministry team saw the widest swing in public opinion possible. Paul's "approval rating" went from being an object of worship (vv. 11–12) to being a victim of stoning (v. 19)! Unbelieving Jews had literally followed Paul all the way from Antioch in their effort to silence his message, and they provoked the citizens of Lystra to stone him.

Later, Paul recounted this season to his son in the ministry.

MISSIONS INSIGHT FROM LYSTRA

Their ministry in the city of Lystra teaches us that missionaries are sometimes required to endure great **persecution**: "having stoned Paul, drew him out of the city, supposing he had been dead" (v. 19).

LESSON ELEVEN—MISSIONS MAKES A DIFFERENCE

2 TIMOTHY 3:11

11 *Persecutions, afflictions, which came unto me at Antioch, at Iconium, at Lystra; what persecutions I endured: but out of them all the Lord delivered me.*

F. Derbe (vv. 14:20–21)

ACTS 14:20–21

20 *Howbeit, as the disciples stood round about him, he rose up, and came into the city: and the next day he departed with Barnabas to Derbe.*

21 *And when they had preached the gospel to that city, and had taught many, they returned again to Lystra, and to Iconium, and Antioch,*

We're not sure how Barnabas escaped the same fate as Paul in Lystra. But after Paul recovered from having been stoned (they thought he was dead, or they wouldn't have stopped the stoning), he reunited with Barnabas and quickly traveled to the nearby city of Derbe.

Preaching and teaching go hand in hand in the work of winning people to Christ and grounding them in the faith. In fact, in all great preaching, teaching is present. Notice that teaching and preaching were major parts of the ministry of the Lord Jesus and later of the Apostle Paul.

MATTHEW 11:1

1 *And it came to pass, when Jesus had made an end of commanding his twelve disciples, he departed thence to* **teach** *and to* **preach** *in their cities.*

MISSIONS INSIGHT FROM DERBE

Their ministry in the city of Derbe teaches the ministry **pattern** *of Paul and Barnabas: "preached...and had taught many" (v. 21).*

179

ACTS 28:31

*31 **Preaching** the kingdom of God, and **teaching** those things which concern the Lord Jesus Christ, with all confidence, no man forbidding him.*

III. The Churches the Missionaries Established

After the preaching, the traveling, the miracles, the long days, and even the stoning, their work was not done. Beginning with Derbe, Paul and Barnabas worked their way back, in reverse order (yes, to the same cities where their lives were threatened!), to make sure these new congregations were firmly established.

A. They taught the new believers in the churches.

ACTS 14:21–22

21 And when they had preached the gospel to that city, and had taught many, they returned again to Lystra, and to Iconium, and Antioch,

22 Confirming the souls of the disciples, and exhorting them to continue in the faith, and that we must through much tribulation enter into the kingdom of God.

Once someone has received Christ as Saviour, the real work of discipling, training, and mentoring begins. Just as parents of a newborn child must exercise great care in nurturing the growth of their baby, so must mature Christians come alongside newborn believers, helping them in their newfound faith. May we be a church to whom God can entrust baby Christians, knowing that

LESSON ELEVEN—MISSIONS MAKES A DIFFERENCE

they will be encouraged in their walk and grounded in their faith. This discipling became a core characteristic of Paul's church planting ministry.

1 THESSALONIANS 2:7–8, 11

7   But we were gentle among you, even as a nurse cherisheth her children:

8   So being affectionately desirous of you, we were willing to have imparted unto you, not the gospel of God only, but also our own souls, because ye were dear unto us.

11   As ye know how we exhorted and comforted and charged every one of you, as a father doth his children,

B. They trained the new pastors in the churches.

ACTS 14:23

23   And when they had ordained them elders in every church, and had prayed with fasting, they commended them to the Lord, on whom they believed.

The work of the New Testament missionary is to train a replacement. Once a church has been planted and established, the leader must reproduce himself in the life of another so that the missionary may move on to plant additional works. This is consistent with the principle that Paul later articulated to Timothy.

2 TIMOTHY 2:2

2   And the things that thou hast heard of me among many witnesses, the same commit thou to faithful men, who shall be able to teach others also.

C. They traveled back to the church that sent them.

ACTS 14:26–28

26 And thence sailed to Antioch, from whence they had been recommended to the grace of God for the work which they fulfilled.

27 And when they were come, and had gathered the church together, they rehearsed all that God had done with them, and how he had opened the door of faith unto the Gentiles.

28 And there they abode long time with the disciples.

A great benefit of supporting missionaries is meeting and hearing from these heroes of the faith, who are being used of God in far away places. The concept of missionaries returning to their sending and supporting churches to give a report of what God accomplished finds its biblical roots here in the closing verses of Acts 14.

Notice in verse 27 that God received the glory for what had been accomplished through this first missionary journey: *"they rehearsed all that God had done."* This was the work of *God*, not the work of Paul and Barnabas.

2 CORINTHIANS 4:7

7 But we have this treasure in earthen vessels, that the excellency of the power may be of God, and not of us.

Conclusion

May we continue to send and support missionaries increasingly with each passing year. And may each of us determine to *be missionaries* ourselves for the Lord Jesus Christ.

LESSON ELEVEN—MISSIONS MAKES A DIFFERENCE

Study Questions

1. Do you have to go to a foreign field to be a missionary?
    No, we are to be missionaries everywhere we go, because all people need the Lord, not just those overseas.

2. Describe the character of the missionaries.
    These men were faithful in the church, they fasted and prayed, and they were filled the Holy Spirit.

3. Who were the first two New Testament missionaries?
    Paul and Barnabas

4. From what city were Paul and Barnabas sent?
    They were sent from Antioch.

5. Who enabled Paul to be in the ministry?
    Jesus Christ

6. What is the great foundation for all Christian ministry?
    Prayer

7. Name the six cities the missionaries reached.
    Salamis, Paphos, Antioch, Iconium, Lystra, and Derbe

8. According to John 15, how can we be filled with the Spirit?
    By abiding with Christ in prayer and in the Word; emptying yourself of sin, pride, and self; asking Christ to fill you; yielding yourself to His control (John 15:1–8)

MAKING A DIFFERENCE

9. What does Paul and Barnabas' ministry in Lystra teach us?
We are sometimes required to endure great persecution.

10. After establishing churches in these cities, Paul and Barnabas went back to the churches. What did they do to make sure the believers were grounded?
They taught the new believers and trained the new pastors.

Memory Verse

2 TIMOTHY 2:2

2 And the things that thou hast heard of me among many witnesses, the same commit thou to faithful men, who shall be able to teach others also.

LESSON TWELVE

Co-Laborers Make
a Difference

Key Verses

Acts 15:40–16:34

Lesson Theme

To make a difference, we must partner with God, His leaders, and His people to take the Gospel to those who need it.

Lesson Overview

We have learned several distinct characteristics of the first-century Christians that enabled them to make a difference in their generation. Our previous lesson revealed the difference Paul and Barnabas made on their first missionary journey. We learned that godly men and women must faithfully carry the Gospel to those who have not yet heard.

We will now fast-forward to the second missionary journey of the Apostle Paul, recorded mostly in Acts 16. The details, as well as the impact, of this particular missionary endeavor are miraculous. An entire region of the world would hear about the saving grace of Jesus Christ because of the work accomplished during this journey.

185

Teaching Outline

I. The Men Who Co-Labored
   A. Silas, the gentle follower
   B. Timothy, the growing convert
   C. Luke, the Greek physician

II. The Macedonian Call
   A. God's leadership required patience.
   B. God's leadership included a petition.
   C. God's leadership required partners.

III. The Multitudes Who Were Converted
   A. A business woman and her friends
   B. A troubled woman who was freed
   C. A prison guard with his family

LESSON TWELVE

Co-Laborers Make
a Difference

Text

Acts 15:40–16:34

Introduction

The fruit of Paul's second missionary journey was phenomenal—lives were transformed, churches were established, miracles were performed, and the kingdom of God was expanded. In this lesson, we will focus not so much on Paul but on his co-laborers.

That which is true today was also true in the first century: without a host of devoted co-laborers, not much will be accomplished in the work of God. Paul made a regular habit of referencing his co-laborers in the letters he wrote.

2 Corinthians 8:23
23 **Titus**, he is my partner and fellowhelper concerning you:

Philippians 2:25
25 **Epaphroditus**, my brother, and companion in labour, and fellowsoldier, but your messenger, and he that ministered to my wants.

Philippians 4:3
3 Help those **women** which laboured with me in the gospel, with **Clement** also, and with other my fellowlabourers.

Colossians 4:7
7 **Tychicus**…who is a beloved brother, and a faithful minister and fellowservant in the Lord:

Colossians 4:11
11 **Justus**…these only are my fellowworkers unto the kingdom of God, which have been a comfort unto me.

1 Thessalonians 3:2
2 And sent **Timotheus**, our brother, and minister of God, and our fellowlabourer in the gospel of Christ

Philemon 1
1 Unto **Philemon** our dearly beloved, and fellowlabourer,

Philemon 24
24 **Marcus, Aristarchus, Demas, Lucas**, my fellowlabourers.

A spiritual leader can only accomplish his task if godly co-laborers will aid him in the ministry. Someone once said, "If you think you're leading, and you look over your shoulder to find no one following, then you're just taking a walk!"

LESSON TWELVE—CO-LABORERS MAKE A DIFFERENCE

Illustration

John Wooden is one of college basketball's most admired and respected coaches. During his successful coaching career at UCLA, *Sports Illustrated* featured a photo of Wooden with this caption: "The guy who puts the ball through the hoop has ten hands." Wooden also said, "The main ingredient to stardom is the rest of the team."

Here in Acts 16, we learn from Paul's companions *three perspectives on co-laboring.*

I.   The Men Who Co-Labored

Let's take a closer look at the three specific men who co-labored with Paul on this second missionary journey.

A. Silas, the gentle follower

When Paul and Barnabas parted ways over their disagreement concerning John Mark (15:39), Paul handpicked Silas to be his traveling companion. This tells us that, in Paul's eyes, Silas was dependable.

ACTS 15:40

40 And Paul chose Silas, and departed, being recommended by the brethren unto the grace of God.

The apostles sent Silas from Jerusalem to help spread the message of the Jerusalem Council (Acts 15) that Gentiles need not come under the ceremonial traditions of the Jews.

How interesting to note that while Paul seems to be an out-in-front pioneer, Silas appears to serve in more of a behind-the-scenes support role. In fact, his name

189

appears thirteen times in the New Testament (Acts 15–18), and in none of those places is he mentioned alone. He is always with another leader like Paul or Barnabas and, later, Timothy.

For Silas, it didn't matter what position he played on the team. He was just thankful to be on the team. Do you have the spiritual maturity to serve in a Silas-like role?

PROVERBS 20:6
6   *Most men will proclaim every one his own goodness: but a faithful man who can find?*

B. Timothy, the growing convert

ACTS 16:1–3
1   *Then came he to Derbe and Lystra: and, behold, a certain disciple was there, named Timotheus, the son of a certain woman, which was a Jewess, and believed; but his father was a Greek:*
2   *Which was well reported of by the brethren that were at Lystra and Iconium.*
3   *Him would Paul have to go forth with him; and took and circumcised him because of the Jews which were in those quarters: for they knew all that his father was a Greek.*

Timothy was saved on Paul's first missionary journey—the time he was stoned and left for dead outside Lystra. In Paul's absence, Timothy had made considerable progress in his Christian walk. Verse 2 tells us that he had a good testimony with the other Christians in his community.

Timothy's father was a Gentile and his mother a Jew, their ethnicity engendering dissension in both groups. Paul's mode of operation as he evangelized city-to-city was to start with the Jews. So to avoid a potential stumbling

LESSON TWELVE—CO-LABORERS MAKE A DIFFERENCE

block, he asked Timothy to be circumcised. Timothy's submission to this request is a tribute to his maturity. He did not demand justification for this Jewish custom. Timothy complied to serve with Paul; it was a simple decision.

In verses 4–6, we learn that Paul, Silas, and Timothy traveled throughout Asia Minor (modern-day Turkey) to many of the churches established on Paul's first missionary journey and that these churches were strengthened by the team's visits.

"There's a difference between interest and commitment. When you are interested in doing something, you do it when it is convenient. When you are committed to something, you accept no excuses."

—Ken Blanchard

Notice what Paul wrote to Timothy later in his personal letter. Apparently, Timothy was already demonstrating character early in his ministry.

1 TIMOTHY 4:12

12 Let no man despise thy youth; but be thou an example of the believers, in word, in conversation, in charity, in spirit, in faith, in purity.

C. Luke, the Greek physician

ACTS 16:10

10 And after he had seen the vision, immediately we endeavoured to go into Macedonia, assuredly gathering that the Lord had called us for to preach the gospel unto them.

In a subtle but clear reference, we learn that Luke joined Paul, Silas, and Timothy on their journey during their time in Troas. The wording from verse 8 to verse 10 changes from *they* to *we*.

God was preparing this group to reach an entirely Gentile culture with the Gospel, and Luke, a Gentile himself, would be a wonderful addition to the missionary team.

We read of Luke's continued companionship with Paul in Colossians 4:14 and Philemon 24. Even years later, when Paul wrote to Timothy, Luke was still co-laboring with him.

2 Timothy 4:11A
11A Only Luke is with me...

II. The Macedonian Call

Acts 16:6–12

6 Now when they had gone throughout Phrygia and the region of Galatia, and were forbidden of the Holy Ghost to preach the word in Asia,

7 After they were come to Mysia, they assayed to go into Bithynia: but the Spirit suffered them not.

8 And they passing by Mysia came down to Troas.

9 And a vision appeared to Paul in the night; There stood a man of Macedonia, and prayed him, saying, Come over into Macedonia, and help us.

10 And after he had seen the vision, immediately we endeavoured to go into Macedonia, assuredly gathering that the Lord had called us for to preach the gospel unto them.

11 Therefore loosing from Troas, we came with a straight course to Samothracia, and the next day to Neapolis;

12 And from thence to Philippi, which is the chief city of that part of Macedonia, and a colony: and we were in that city abiding certain days.

LESSON TWELVE—CO-LABORERS MAKE A DIFFERENCE

In verse 9, Paul received a call to Macedonia. This unexpected directive thrust the Gospel forward into Europe. Notice how God's leadership was carefully exercised in the lives of Paul and his co-laborers.

A. God's leadership required patience.

Paul, though an aggressive leader, remained sensitive to the voice of God's Spirit. The pull of his heart in verse 6 was to remain in Asia Minor to reach those cities he was unable to enter on their first journey. Then, when God's Spirit did not give him peace about that, he thought of those cities in the Northern region called Bithynia (v. 7), but again God's Spirit said, "No."

God had a different timetable for taking the Gospel into Asia. The Bible tells us in Acts 19:10 that, as a result of Paul's third missionary journey, the Gospel reached that part of the world. God knows the end from the beginning (Isaiah 46:10), and His plan is perfect.

PSALM 37:23
23 *The steps of a good man are ordered by the LORD: and he delighteth in his way.*

PROVERBS 3:5–6
5 *Trust in the LORD with all thine heart; and lean not unto thine own understanding.*
6 *In all thy ways acknowledge him, and he shall direct thy paths.*

Commentary on Acts 16:6–8

Silas and Timothy must have wondered what was going on. They had been prepared for

MAKING A DIFFERENCE

tremendous bursts of activity, for mass meetings, wholesale conversions, bitter opposition, for stripes and imprisonment, for apostolic miracles, for hairbreadth escapes. They had expected to see a trail of churches strung out behind them in Phrygia, Asia, Bithynia, and Mysia. But there was nothing. Was this Paul's usual way of carrying on? Surely there was more to it than this aimless drifting from place to place. Had Paul lost his nerve? They had expected almost anything but this uncertainty, this constant tramping the highways for hundreds of miles with nothing to show for it but Paul's vetoing of every suggestion that they stop here and get to work.—*Exploring Acts,* by John Phillips, Loizeaux 1986

God is in charge. He doesn't owe us an explanation, and if we trust His leadership, His work *will* be accomplished and circumstances will work together for our good and His glory.

In what area of your life is He guiding you? To what is God saying, *"No! I know you don't understand, but trust Me."* God primarily speaks to His people today through His Word, His people, and His Holy Spirit. I encourage you to carefully listen, trust Him, and follow His leading.

B. God's leadership included a petition.

In verse 8, Paul had arrived at Troas, doing his best to follow the leadership of the Holy Spirit but wondering exactly where the Lord would open a door to advance the Gospel. Then, the light came on, and God spoke!

The vision that appeared to Paul came in the form of a petition—a call for help. Often God disguises His best opportunities as needs. Do you notice the needs that cross your path? Are you alert to needs? We live in a needy world. The man who seeks to meet spiritual needs through the power of the Holy Spirit will never have trouble staying busy in service to Christ.

1 John 3:17

17   But whoso hath this world's good, and seeth his brother have need, and shutteth up his bowels of compassion from him, how dwelleth the love of God in him?

Because Paul was sensitive and responsive to this call, the next leg of his missionary endeavor came into focus. The Gospel would cross the threshold of Europe for the first time. Paul and his companions followed the call to Macedonia where they won souls, established churches, and trained leaders, claiming a continent for Christ. And it all started with a man and his co-laborers who responded to a petition for help.

C. God's leadership required partners.

Leaders discover biblical vision in God's Word. Whenever God grants vision to the man of God, He couples with it an opportunity for the people of God to follow and support that vision.

Pay special attention to the pronouns used in verse 10: *"And after **he** had seen the vision, immediately **we** endeavoured to go into Macedonia, assuredly gathering that the Lord had called **us**...."*

The Lord had already revealed to Silas, Timothy, and Luke that it was His will for them to labor with Paul. So when Paul shared the vision, they followed with joy and enthusiasm. We are taught in the Word of God to "follow the faith" of God's appointed leaders.

Hebrews 13:7

7   Remember them which have the rule over you, who have spoken unto you the word of God: whose faith follow, considering the end of their conversation.

III. The Multitudes Who Were Converted

Because of a leader willing to follow God's call, and because of co-laborers willing to join him in the work, many received Christ. We will not know the extent of these conversions until we reach Heaven, but chapter 16 provides a glimpse at several whose lives were touched.

A. A business woman and her friends

Acts 16:14–15

14   And a certain woman named Lydia, a seller of purple, of the city of Thyatira, which worshipped God, heard us: whose heart the Lord opened, that she attended unto the things which were spoken of Paul.

15   And when she was baptized, and her household, she besought us, saying, If ye have judged me to be faithful to the Lord, come into my house, and abide there. And she constrained us.

> "When God calls a leader, He always supplies the followers."
> —Curtis Hutson

God is always at work in hearts, preparing them to receive the Gospel. Verse 14 tells us He opened Lydia's heart. Even today, He opens the hearts of searching people. And He continues to lead his children across their paths, to share His love. Will you allow Him to use you, to speak to someone whose heart He is opening now?

LESSON TWELVE—CO-LABORERS MAKE A DIFFERENCE

COLOSSIANS 4:3

3 *Withal praying also for us, that God would open unto us a door of utterance, to speak the mystery of Christ, for which I am also in bonds:*

B. A troubled woman who was freed

ACTS 16:16–18

16 *And it came to pass, as we went to prayer, a certain damsel possessed with a spirit of divination met us, which brought her masters much gain by soothsaying:*

17 *The same followed Paul and us, and cried, saying, These men are the servants of the most high God, which shew unto us the way of salvation.*

18 *And this did she many days. But Paul, being grieved, turned and said to the spirit, I command thee in the name of Jesus Christ to come out of her. And he came out the same hour.*

Though not to the same degree as *this* woman, all men and women are in bondage to sin. And their bondage includes a death sentence. We cannot free them by our own power, but as co-laborers with God and His people, we can deliver the message that frees them.

JOHN 8:36

36 *If the Son therefore shall make you free, ye shall be free indeed.*

C. A prison guard with his family

ACTS 16:26–32

26 *And suddenly there was a great earthquake, so that the foundations of the prison were shaken: and immediately all the doors were opened, and every one's bands were loosed.*

197

27 And the keeper of the prison awaking out of his sleep, and seeing the prison doors open, he drew out his sword, and would have killed himself, supposing that the prisoners had been fled.

28 But Paul cried with a loud voice, saying, Do thyself no harm: for we are all here.

29 Then he called for a light, and sprang in, and came trembling, and fell down before Paul and Silas,

30 And brought them out, and said, Sirs, what must I do to be saved?

31 And they said, Believe on the Lord Jesus Christ, and thou shalt be saved, and thy house.

32 And they spake unto him the word of the Lord, and to all that were in his house.

Freeing a demon-possessed young woman had landed Paul and Silas in jail. But even in their hour of affliction, they prayed and sang. They could have just as easily questioned God and complained. But they were familiar with Jesus' exhortation.

MATTHEW 5:11–12

11 Blessed are ye, when men shall revile you, and persecute you, and shall say all manner of evil against you falsely, for my sake.

12 Rejoice, and be exceeding glad: for great is your reward in heaven: for so persecuted they the prophets which were before you.

Because Paul and Silas prayed and sang, they were given the opportunity—through a miracle earthquake—to share the Gospel with the keeper of the prison. The story goes on to explain that not only the guard but also his entire family were saved and baptized.

LESSON TWELVE—CO-LABORERS MAKE A DIFFERENCE

Conclusion

Think of all that was accomplished in the kingdom of God and for the glory of God, because God's people determined to labor together. God opened the door to take the Gospel into Europe. Souls were saved and lives were transformed.

Similarly, God has opened a door of opportunity for us today. The issue is whether we will stand on the sideline or get involved as co-laborers in the work of God!

Study Questions

1. To what region were the missionaries headed when Paul saw the vision and received the call to go to Macedonia?
Bithynia

2. What three men co-labored with Paul on his second missionary journey?
Silas, Timothy, and Luke

3. Which one of these co-laborers was saved on Paul's first missionary journey?
Timothy

4. What type of laborer was Silas?
A behind-the-scenes laborer, not being concerned with who was out in front as long as the work got done

5. In reference to the Macedonian call, name three aspects of God's leadership in Paul's life.
It required patience.

It included a petition.

It required partners.

6. Is the Holy Spirit trying to guide you in a particular area today? Will you trust His leadership in your life?
Answers will vary.

7. How does God often disguise His best opportunities?
As needs

LESSON TWELVE—CO-LABORERS MAKE A DIFFERENCE

8. Name some of the people who were converted on this
    missionary journey.
    *The businesswoman Lydia, a possessed damsel, a prison
    guard and his family*

9. Why did Paul and Silas end up in jail?
    *They were thrown into jail because the demon-possessed
    woman was saved, and therefore was of no use to her
    masters, making them angry.*

10. Would Paul's ministry have been as fruitful without his
    co-laborers? Why or why not?
    *No, he would not have been as effective on his missionary
    journey. When God calls a man to the work of God, He
    always supplies the co-laborers to come alongside and
    help. Teamwork makes the dream work.*

Memory Verse

PROVERBS 20:6
*6 Most men will proclaim every one his own goodness: but a
faithful man who can find?*

LESSON THIRTEEN

Commitment Makes a Difference

Key Verses

Acts 20:17–24

Lesson Theme

To make a difference, we must remain committed to the cause of Jesus Christ and to His will for our lives.

Lesson Overview

We have learned from the first-century Christians how we can make a difference. We will now focus on the ministry of the Apostle Paul. From Paul's first journey we learned that *missions* makes a difference. From his second journey we learned that *co-laborers* make a difference. Today we will learn from Paul's third and final missionary journey that *commitment* makes a difference.

Teaching Outline

I. Paul's Attitude
   A. He would not allow adverse circumstances to move him.
   B. He would not allow the attacks of critics to move him.

II. Paul's Abandon
   A. His motive for abandon
   B. His method of abandon
   C. His Model for abandon

III. Paul's Aim
   A. The goal of Paul's aim
   B. The Giver of Paul's aim
   C. The greatness of Paul's aim

LESSON THIRTEEN

Commitment Makes
a Difference

Text

Acts 20:17–24

Introduction:

As a roaring lion, the devil seeks to tear godly people from
their spiritual goals. But the Christian who is truly committed
will not be moved.

> **DEFINITION**
>
> **Commitment:** *The state of being bound emotionally or
> intellectually to an ideal or course of action.—Webster's II New
> College Dictionary, 1999*

MAKING A DIFFERENCE

PSALM 16:8
*8 I have set the LORD always before me: because he is at my
right hand, I shall not be moved.*

A person who has bound himself to an object cannot
move from that object. If I handcuff myself to a briefcase,
that briefcase is going wherever I go. It is committed—or
bound—to me. Our Lord is looking for people who will bind
themselves to His will and purpose for their lives.
Paul bound himself to the work and will of God. From
his life, we learn that by demonstrating commitment we
can make a difference. Verse 24 uncovers *three aspects of
Paul's commitment.*

I.   Paul's Attitude
"But none of these things move me…"

A. He would not allow adverse circumstances to move him.

Paul faced tremendous adversity. Laboring as a pioneering
Christian missionary during the first century was not an
easy task.

2 CORINTHIANS 11:23–28
*23 Are they ministers of Christ? (I speak as a fool) I am
more; in labours more abundant, in stripes above measure,
in prisons more frequent, in deaths oft.*
24 Of the Jews five times received I forty stripes save one.
*25 Thrice was I beaten with rods, once was I stoned, thrice
I suffered shipwreck, a night and a day I have been in
the deep;*

206

LESSON THIRTEEN—COMMITMENT MAKES A DIFFERENCE

26 In journeyings often, in perils of waters, in perils of robbers, in perils by mine own countrymen, in perils by the heathen, in perils in the city, in perils in the wilderness, in perils in the sea, in perils among false brethren;
27 In weariness and painfulness, in watchings often, in hunger and thirst, in fastings often, in cold and nakedness.
28 Beside those things that are without, that which cometh upon me daily, the care of all the churches.

Paul had learned how to keep the winds of adversity from blowing him off course. How? His life was anchored to the Rock, Jesus Christ (see Hebrews 6:19 and 1 Corinthians 10:4)!

2 CORINTHIANS 4:16
16 For which cause we faint not; but though our outward man perish, yet the inward man is renewed day by day."

PSALM 62:6
6 He only is my rock and my salvation: he is my defence; I shall not be moved.

Illustration

William Hutchinson Murray was an internationally recognized mountain climber in Europe, both before and after World War II. During the war he was imprisoned by the Nazis, as a result of using his climbing skills for the Allied Forces. In his 1951 book, *The Scottish Himalayan Expedition,* Murray explained commitment in this way: "Until I am committed, there is a hesitancy— a chance to draw back. But the moment I definitely commit myself, then God moves also and a whole stream of events erupts. All manner of unforeseen incidents, meetings, persons, and material assistance which I could never have dreamed would have come my way begin to flow toward me the moment I make a commitment."

B. He would not allow the attacks of critics to move him.

Living for God without apology positions you as a target for ridicule. Sadly, some Christians who once stood boldly for Christ have crumbled under the pressure around them.

In many of his letters, Paul found it necessary to defend himself from people who had gone to *his* converts and questioned his motives, integrity, and doctrine. He described ungodly attacks:

"It's human to stand with the crowd, but it's divine to stand alone. It's manlike to follow the people and drift with the tide, but it's God-like to follow the principle and to stem the tide. It's natural to compromise conscience, and follow the social and religious fashion for the sake of gain and pleasure, but it's divine to sacrifice both on the altar of truth and duty."

—Author Unknown

ACTS 21:27

27 And when the seven days were almost ended, the Jews which were of Asia, when they saw him in the temple, stirred up all the people, and laid hands on him,

2 TIMOTHY 4:16–17

16 At my first answer no man stood with me, but all men forsook me: I pray God that it may not be laid to their charge.

17 Notwithstanding the Lord stood with me, and strengthened me; that by me the preaching might be fully known, and that all the Gentiles might hear: and I was delivered out of the mouth of the lion."

208

Lesson Thirteen—Commitment Makes a Difference

Moving in the opposite direction of mainstream society always creates friction. When you encounter adverse circumstances or the attacks of critics as you are traveling down the highway of the Christian life, don't look for "EXIT" signs!

II. Paul's Abandon

"…neither count I my life dear unto myself…"

All of us are, by nature, self-centered. We tend to "look out for number one," but this philosophy runs contrary to what Jesus taught. Paul overcame this tendency by *abandoning* himself.

A. His motive for abandon

In a word, Paul's motive was *others*. *Abandon* means dedicating my life to Jesus Christ and to the others He has called me to serve or reach. *Abandon* means forgetting about my own personal needs or desires and seeking the good of others.

Mark 8:35

35 For whosoever will save his life shall lose it; but whosoever shall lose his life for my sake and the gospel's, the same shall save it."

Illustration

A veteran Coast Guard officer in Florida gave the command for one of the new recruits to follow him to the rescue boat. The new sailor hesitated, "The storm is

MAKING A DIFFERENCE

so large, we may never come back!" To this the officer replied, "Our duty is not to *come back*, but to *go out*."

Moses abandoned himself, motivated by a desire to help his Hebrew brothers and sisters.

HEBREWS 11:24–25

24 By faith Moses, when he was come to years, refused to be called the son of Pharaoh's daughter;
25 Choosing rather to suffer affliction with the people of God, than to enjoy the pleasures of sin for a season;

B. His method of abandon

The method we must follow is *death to self.* Paul simply said, *"I die daily"* (1 Corinthians 15:31).

The only way we will be able to truly abandon our own wishes, wants, and concerns is if we crucify our flesh. You see, a dead man cannot look out for himself!

> *"In reading the lives of great men, I've found that the first great victory they won was over themselves."*
> —President Harry Truman

GALATIANS 2:20

20 I am crucified with Christ: nevertheless I live; yet not I, but Christ liveth in me: and the life which I now live in the flesh I live by the faith of the Son of God, who loved me, and gave himself for me.

Illustration

Amy Carmichael helped neglected and abused children on the mission field of India for fifty-six years without a furlough. Her prayer was:

210

LESSON THIRTEEN—COMMITMENT MAKES A DIFFERENCE

God, harden me against myself,
The coward with pathetic voice
Who craves for ease and rest and joy.
Myself, arch-traitor to myself,
My hollowest friend,
My deadliest foe,
My clog, whatever road I go.

C. His Model for abandon

Jesus Christ served as Paul's model—and ours today—of the life of true abandon.

MATTHEW 20:28

28 Even as the Son of man came not to be ministered unto, but to minister, and to give his life a ransom for many.

Then He asked us to do the same:

LUKE 9:23

23 And he said to them all, If any man will come after me, let him deny himself, and take up his cross daily, and follow me.

The work of the Lord must come before our personal comfort.

III. Paul's Aim

"...so that I might finish my course with joy, and the ministry, which I have received of the Lord Jesus, to testify the gospel of the grace of God."

A. The goal of Paul's aim

"...so that I might finish my course with joy..."

> *"To finish first, you must first finish."*
> —Rick Mears, Indy 500 Race Car Driver

Many people start well, but few finish well. Such is the case with Bible characters, political leaders, and of course, twenty-first century Christians. Paul told the Ephesian elders of his desire to finish well. Years later, he was able to testify to Timothy that he was nearing this finish line.

2 TIMOTHY 4:7

7 *I have fought a good fight, I have finished my course, I have kept the faith:*

> *"A hero is no braver than an ordinary man, but he is brave five minutes longer."* —Ralph Waldo Emerson

Don't let *your own* failures along the way cause you to quit. Tracy Mullins wrote that when it comes to failure for the Christian, he must realize four things: God expects it (Psalm 103:14 and Hebrews 4:15). God forgives it (Isaiah 30:18). God uses it (Jonah 3). God sees past it (Hebrews 11).

B. The Giver of Paul's aim

"...the ministry, which I have received of the Lord Jesus..."

Our calling to commitment comes directly from our Saviour, Jesus Christ. Jesus has apprehended us (or taken hold of us) for His work. And our response must be to apprehend that work.

LESSON THIRTEEN—COMMITMENT MAKES A DIFFERENCE

PHILIPPIANS 3:13–14

13 Brethren, I count not myself to have apprehended: but this one thing I do, forgetting those things which are behind, and reaching forth unto those things which are before,
14 I press toward the mark for the prize of the high calling of God in Christ Jesus.

C. The greatness of Paul's aim

"… to testify the gospel of the grace of God."

Telling folks about the good news of God's grace is the greatest thing to which we can commit ourselves.

ROMANS 10:1

1 Brethren, my heart's desire and prayer to God for Israel is, that they might be saved.

LUKE 19:10

10 For the Son of man is come to seek and to save that which was lost.

We have the opportunity to invest our lives, as Paul did, in the Gospel. Regardless of your career field, you regularly come in contact with people who need the Lord. Don't miss out on the greatest calling known to mankind—sharing Jesus Christ with others.

Conclusion

For what particular purpose has God called you? What has He given you to accomplish? Is it being a godly spouse, a Christ-honoring parent, a soulwinner, a servant in His work, a Bible student, a prayer warrior? Whatever it is, accept it, realize it's from Him, and finish it!

Illustration

The Texas war for independence from Mexico raged in 1836. Dictator Santa Anna declared as his goal the extinction of Texas. The Texans won the war, but not without grave losses, including the Alamo, a mission just outside of the city of San Antonio.

When Santa Anna captured San Antonio, 188 Texans fled to this mission. The Texans fought off the Mexican army for nearly two weeks. Their requests for support were continually unsuccessful, and their defeat by Santa Anna's army of 3,000 appeared inevitable.

General William B. Travis was forced to deliver the news that no help was coming. On March 3, he said, "Our fate is sealed. Within a very few days—perhaps a few hours—we must all be in eternity. This is our destiny and we cannot avoid it. This is our certain doom."

He explained that escape was still possible, but said, "For myself, I will fight as long as there is a breath in my body." He then drew a line in the sand with his sword, and said, "I want every man who is determined to stay here with me and die, to cross this line."

In a solid row, all of the men, including Davy Crockett, stepped forward, with two exceptions. One was Jim Bowie who lay on a cot from previous injuries. He asked the others to carry him across the line in the sand. The other, a French mercenary fighting only for money, fled. What the 186 men who stepped across the line demonstrated that day was *commitment*.

I wonder if Jesus Christ were to draw a line in the sand, asking for *my* commitment, would I cross it? Would *you*?

LESSON THIRTEEN—COMMITMENT MAKES A DIFFERENCE

Study Questions

Acts 20:17-24

1. According to *Webster's Dictionary,* what is the definition of commitment? *quality of being dedicated to a cause, activity etc.*
The state of being bound emotionally or intellectually to an ideal or course of action.
2. an engagement or obligation that restricts freedom of action. *Affliction*

2. Name three aspects of Paul's commitment. *II Cor 3:23-28*
He had the right attitude. *2 Cor 4:16, Psalm 16:8*
He abandoned self. *Gal. 2:20*

   He aimed to finish his course with joy. *Phil 3:13-14*

3. How was Paul able to say, *"But none of these things move me…"*?
Answers will vary. He was anchored in the Lord Jesus Christ, and didn't let his circumstances get him off track.

4. According to 2 Corinthians 4:16, what is to be renewed day by day?
Our inward man

5. What motivated Paul for complete abandonment of self?
Others

6. Paul's method of abandon was death to self. What verses support that concept?
First Corinthians 15:31 and Galatians 2:20, among others

Commitment- def 2 -*
Paul example
Neil Degrass⇒ real followers

MAKING A DIFFERENCE

7. Who was Paul's model for abandoning self, and how did He model abandonment?
Jesus Christ was Paul's model, and He modeled abandonment by going to the Cross for us.

8. What goal was the aim of Paul's life?
That he might finish his course with joy.

9. How committed are you to the Lord Jesus Christ? Are you in danger of anything "moving you"?
Answers will vary.

Memory Verse

2 TIMOTHY 4:7

7   *I have fought a good fight, I have finished my course, I have kept the faith:*

For additional Christian
growth resources visit
www.strivingtogether.com